D0841710

Who Do You Think You Are?

Reflections of a Writer's Life

Joseph Torra

Who Do You Think You Are?
Reflections of a Writer's Life

© Joseph Torra 2021

PFP Publishing
PO Box 829 - Byfield, MA 01922
ISBN: 978-1-7367202-1-9

(also available in eBook and hardcover formats)

cover image © Joseph Torra

Publisher's Cataloging-In-Publication Data
(Prepared by The Donohue Group, Inc.)

Names: Torra, Joseph, 1955- author.
Title: Who do you think you are? : reflections of a writer's
    life / Joseph Torra.
Description: Byfield, MA : PFP Publishing, [2021]
Identifiers: ISBN 9781736720226 (hardcover) | ISBN
    9781736720219 (paperback)
Subjects: LCSH: Torra, Joseph, 1955- | Authors, Ameri-
    can--20th century--Biography. | Manic-depressive
    persons--Massachusetts--Biography. | LCGFT: Auto-
    biographies.
Classification: LCC PS3570.O688 Z46 2021 | DDC 813.54
    B--dc23

Books by Joseph Torra

Fiction

My Ground Trilogy:
Gas Station
Tony Luongo
My Ground

What's So Funny
Call Me Waiter
They Say
The Bystander's Scrapbook
What it Takes

Poetry

Time Being
Duck Tour: The Movie
Keep Watching the Sky
After the Chinese
Domino Sessions
Sixteen Paintings
Watteau Sky
August Letter to My Wife and Daughters

Praise for Torra's Work

"It takes a lot of skill to break the rules (or invent them) without confusing, annoying or losing readers. Joseph Torra demonstrates gallons of such skill in his first novel. *Gas Station* is a coming-of-age story. It's also a gritty, greasy, gas-fumey slice of a particular way of life. Torra grabs for and catches the essence of this boy's world with flashes, snatches, and flares of thoughts, observations, illuminations bright as welding arcs. What's absolutely fascinating here is not only that the boy sees, but how he sees it, how he connects one image, event, observation to another. *Gas Station* is a wild ride in a fast car fueled by adolescence and souped up with Torra's brave, consistent, highly effective, marvelously, unconventional prose. Torra has also published a collection of poetry: *Keep Watching the Sky*. Readers will to want keep watching for new books by this exceptional writer."

—Rebecca Rule, *Nashua Telegraph*

"His deadpan tone leads to touches of humor and pathos, while his highly compressed prose at times achieve the intensity of poetry."

—*London Observer*

"Torra combines a deep understanding of auto parts with an equally profound grasp of sentence non-structure....If words were lug nuts, he'd spin them in ways the guys down at garage would never dream of."   **—Sally Eckhoff, *New York Times***

"Torra's characters speak in an almost poetic cadence."   **—*Boston Magazine***

"Far from being of fleeting interest, this gas station allows Torra to offer an intricate, sympathetic, sometimes outraged, always graceful commentary on the larger world.... One of the reasons *Gas Station* works so well on a universal level is because it is presented in the plain, unselfconscious voice of a boy on the verge of adolescence—a quiet boy who notices everything.... Mostly, the boy just tries to understand. But when he weighs the dark side related to small-town poverty, there is a hint of incipient outrage.... Yet Torra is not a writer of unrelenting gloom. If he has an overriding theme, it is that, as repetitive, boring and bleak as life is at times, it may also be absurdly funny and touching, even remarkable—especially because of the human urge toward integrity, which Torra presents in the shape of Blackie, the gas station's foul-mouthed but kindly mechanic. ...Blackie offers the boy something his father cannot, a passion for creativity. For true mechanics, Torra suggests, are like poets (which the dreamy boy will surely grow up to be), honest laborers who pay attention to detail, never take short cuts and think out the implications of what they do. In its understated way, *Gas Station* is a celebration of artistic truth, not as something to put on a pedestal, but as a necessity, inextricably entwined with life and hope."

— Charlotte Innes, *Los Angeles Times*

"*The Bystander's Scrapbook* is deceptively simple and highly powerful...A moving and elegant book, the novel illuminates the complexity behind America's image as the 'cradle of democracy' and 'land of the free' " **—*Kirkus UK***

"In *They Say*, the scope of the narrative is as ambitious as it is detailed...Many of these [elements] are common to immigrant literature ...However, the shifting of point of view enables one to see the Pelligrinos as multi-dimensional human beings, individuals rather than types. A composite portrait of the family materializes with each successive account—almost in the way a painting takes shape before the watcher's eye as each brush stroke is added to the canvas. As the welter of vivid detail accumulates, one begins to share an almost unbearable intimacy with these deeply flawed human beings, the story-tellers along with the silent members of the clan. One finds oneself in their imaginations and memories, as well as in their bedrooms and kitchens. The saga of the Pelligrinos stays with its readers long after their voices have fallen silent."

—Angela Alaimo O'Donnell, *Italian Americana*

"The new book by Joseph Torra, *Tony Luongo,* is a brilliant read." **—*UK Esquire***

"Torra writes wonderfully...There are two kinds of writers, those who want to imitate literature, and those who want to imitate life. The second kind are better, and Torra's in the second category. [*Call Me Waiter*] is fast, clear-eyed, full of insider information entertainingly delivered. He's not particularly gentle with his characters, but he approaches them with a matter-of-factness which, however badly they behave, allows them their humanity."

—Daisy Fried, *Poetry Foundation*

"*Gas Station*, like the small town mid-sixties, is populated by underclass alcoholic hangers on, sexist garage guys, a codependent wife, and an abusive boss. But Torra is too sharp a poet to use these reductive words. To paraphrase Joseph Brodsky, pop-psych labels, like evil, are "bad stylists." This is indeed a novel, and a successful one. The singular voice hooks us, time and place are indelibly fixed, and the plot has a literal climax. There's a double loss of innocence in the subtly heartbreaking final chapter, as father and son part ways at the dawning of Watergate and the Age of Aquarius."

— **Marcia Deihl, *Harvard Review***

"In the *My Ground Trilogy*, Torra depicts pride in the job well-done, but also an intensely harsh suffering. He does so in innovative forms—as if John Fante has met Gertrude Stein. Torra's innovations in form are intensely realistic. This boy, man, and woman are neither heroes nor anti-heroes. The books and the lives recorded in them are linked by geography—the edges of Boston and are free from self-righteous morality and ethnic neighborhood sentimentality."

—**Dennis Barone, *Italian Americana***

"Torra makes a visit to the coffee shop and the chat of the mechanics into a kaleidoscope of high poetry in which the rhythms of everyday life are beautiful not banal." —***Guardian***

"Joe Torra uses working-class material to create literary art. His writing has a freshness that is rare in today's world of fiction."

—**Fred Gardaphe, *Annali d'Italianistica***

Best of 1996

Salman Rushdie (Pantheon)

Dark, funny, ribald, richly metaphorical and brilliantly imagined, Rushdie's picaresque novel is a parable of all the paradoxes that are modern India. His story of the rise and fall of an eccentric Portuguese-Indian family of merchants is a chronicle of amorous entanglements, betrayals, artistic ideals, political chicanery, farcical interplay and tragedy.

Last Orders

Graham Swift (Knopf)

Four working-class men meet at their favorite East London pub to carry out the last orders of the man whose ashes they are to scatter by the sea. As their pilgrimage progresses, their tangled relationships and guilty secrets are revealed. Swift plumbs the existential questions of identity while remaining true to the Cockney voices and the social circumstances of his proletarian characters.

Mason's Retreat

Christopher Tilghman (Random)

Elegant prose and a lyrical evocation of Maryland's Eastern Shore distinguish this story of a family whose decision to accept the legacy of their deteriorating ancestral home during the Depression exacerbates the strains between the parents, inflicts ironic burdens on the children and leads to tragedy.

Gas Station

Joseph Torra (Zoland)

In this beautiful first novel, an adolescent boy working at his father's gas station records his experiences of the world and his place in it. The energy with which the the narrator records every detail that catches his attention translates into a stream-of-consciousness riff that is both lyrical and true.

The Laws of Our Fathers

Scott Turow (Farrar, Straus & Giroux)

Whether or not legal experts will agree that his protagonist should have declared a bench trial on the case she is to judge, Turow's new legal thriller succeeds on its considerable literary merits. In its assured depictions of a group of former 1960s student activists brought together by the arrest of a drug lord and the long hand of fate, this rich, complex and moving story is an insightful look at tangled family relationships.

In the Beauty of the Lilies

John Updike (Knopf)

Four generations of an American family-from a minister who loses his faith to his great-grandson who joins a fundamentalist religious cult--populate Updike's ambitious social, cultural and historical panorama. The history of the movie industry, which seemed to promise its own kind of salvation, is woven through the narrative.

To my editors and publishers:
Roland Pease, Ian Preece, Bill Corbett,
Gian Lombardo and Peter Sarno

Torra to read his work

BRATTLEBORO — Joseph Torra will read from his new novel "Gas Station" Thursday at 7:30 p.m. at Collected Works, 29 High St.

☐ BOOK NEWS

JOSEPH TORRA

"Gas Station," which received a starred review in Publishers' Weekly, is the story of an adolescent working in his father's gas station north of Boston, where he gradually comes to learn the rules of politics, sex, business, marriage, the church, and the other forces that matter in his community. The style of Torra's prose is innovative, with trivialities often meeting new realizations in a sentence without punctuation. The reviewer in *Publishers' Weekly* found that "Gas Station grants the whole process a grace that is beautiful without being precious and universal in its specificity."

Joseph Torra took his bachelor of arts and master of arts degrees from the University of Massachusetts in Boston. He has directed several reading series in the Boston area and from 1989 through 1995 was a publisher and editor of the literary magazine Lift. He has done guest lecturing at Northeastern University and other Boston area schools.

Torra's poems have appeared in a number of magazines, including Agni, The Green Mountains Review, and Soundings East. A chapbook, 16 Paintings, appeared from Dromenon Press in 1992. In April he was at Collected Works to read from his book of poems, Keep Watching the Sky.

A reception in the Cafe Beyond will follow the reading.

I'm sitting in a highchair in a dining room. The room full, the mood festive—a holiday, Sunday dinner, maybe a birthday party. People gather around a table talking loudly waving their arms, making sounds that soar high and low driven by alternating rhythmic patterns. It must be Italian, or at least part Italian. All of the family gatherings were made up of my grandparents, aunts and uncles who spoke Italian. My early language orientation consisted of broken English, and a peasant southern Italian dialect—I suppose similar to what is known today in the Hispanic-American culture as Spanglish. It is the first time I am aware of myself as a living being among other living beings. This highchair scene is my first conscious memory. It probably isn't, but over the years my imagination has made it so. I'm alone. Cut off by my lack of verbal skills. I cannot communicate. I see the crowd, hear the din, but cannot understand it nor form words of my own. This image and noise are burned into my imagination. Memory bounces like a pinball back to that highchair.

~

There were no books at 263 Park Street in Medford, the two-family house where I grew up on the first floor. The exception being a Bible that sat inside a cedar box on the dresser in my parents' bedroom. As a boy on a few occasions I removed the book from its wooden box, its sweet cedar smell accompanied my reading *in the beginning God created the world and let there be light* and all of that. I never made it past the opening section, paging ahead to be intimidated by all the writing—so many pages—and there was the *New Testament* and the *Old Testament*. What difference between the two? No matter how hard I tried, what they taught us in Sunday school or what I heard in Mass, I could never differentiate between God, Jesus, and the Holy Ghost. At seven I made my First Holy Communion, and a few years later my Confirmation. When I first opened that Bible, I believed it carried a secret that could transport me beyond the here and now. Surely if I kept reading, the secret would be revealed. One morning I rose early and walked to Saint Francis of Assisi church where we knew all the priests and nuns—where my sisters were married, and my father and mother had their funerals. Inside I marveled at the vastness of the ornate walls lined with plaques depicting the Stations of the Cross, and the brilliantly colored stained-glass windows, and the altar where on Sunday the priest performed his magic. That morning I knelt down at the altar, staring up at the giant crucifix—the perfectly sculpted wooden figure of an oversize Jesus nailed to that cross—his veins and muscles protruding so real, crown of thorns around his head, blood dripping from the wounds. Torture. Below his watchful eyes, beneath burning candles, under the stale smell of incense I prayed. I prayed to God to give me a sign that he was really there. I prayed with my entire being, throwing myself at his mercy, begging for one sign that he existed and watched over me. My mother went to church every Sunday though she never opened the book sitting on her dresser. If I asked her, I'm certain that she wouldn't know the difference between the Father, the Son, and the Holy Ghost. But she was a devout Catholic, had been raised so, and never questioned her faith. She believed fully that there was an all-powerful God in heaven, and when she died, she would be with her mother and dead siblings there. Early on I was drawn to the rituals: the smell of incense burning, hearing the priest speak and sing in Latin, the communion, the ornate dress of the priest and altar boys. Yet eventually they wore thin and became empty to me. In Sunday school on Thursday afternoons after public school, the nuns taught in terms of good and bad. We learned that only Catholics went to heaven. No other religion offered such eternal rewards. Jesus was nailed to the cross—he hung there for three days and died for my sins. By the time I was twelve or so I'd had enough. No matter how hard I tried I received nothing from the Bible or catechism or what the priests and nuns taught me. My prayers went unanswered. All I got from Sunday school was contempt from the nuns because my parents chose to send me to public rather than Catholic school. How could I believe that some guy got nailed to a cross and left to hang for days and when he died, he flew up to heaven? And for my sins? And what about being good so I could go up there for eternity after I died? If they'd lie about Santa Claus, they'd lie about anything.

~

After the Bible I probably would have given up books if not for *The Oxford History of the American People*. It's the 1965 edition. As I write I'm looking at it on a bookshelf in the history section of my library. Inside, on the front page, written when I was ten years old: Joseph Torra/263 Park St./Medford/EX6-9653. It's my very first book, purchased through the mail. I don't know why I had my parents buy it for me. For some reason history interested me way back then. There's a photo of a Benjamin Franklin bust on the title page. I tried to read the book, over a thousand pages. I don't remember how far I made it but probably not very. At first, I was drawn into the discovery of the new world, and Plymouth Plantation and Jamestown, but I got bogged down in specifics. I found the minutiae behind the interesting stuff too overwhelming. But the seed of history had been planted. In high school the only 'A' I ever received for a grade was an American History course. History is about the human condition. Not much different from fiction except with fiction the names, dates and facts can change. Who are we? What makes us do the things we do? How did we get here and why act the way we do? My first college evening course was American History. I received an 'A' there too. I'd been petrified that I couldn't do college level work, and this was a big shot in the arm. I chose history as my first college major before later switching over to English.

~

The great American cultural current swept me away. For me, it's only one generation back to the peasantry of the hills outside Napoli, Italy in the province of Avellino—yet I feel like one of William Carlos Williams's *pure products of America gone crazy*. Once you've gone *there*, you can't go back. In reinventing myself from a kid on the Medford street corner whose parents had been told by my teachers: *teach him a trade he's not very bright*—it's as if I've betrayed those I left behind. In moving on to a new life I feel like an outsider. I have spent most of my adulthood identifying as an artist, but often I've felt like I don't belong. Yet when I find myself back in the old world, among the working class—I automatically hide my education and erudition. I know I am no longer one of them. I know what they will think of me if they find me out. In their world, street smarts are fine, practical wisdom is accepted but too much education and information are a threat. One time my mother visited the first apartment I shared with Molly, later to be my wife. She looked around at all the bookshelves

7

and asked, *what are you going to do with all those books?* I told her I planned on reading them to which she replied, *read them...you'll hurt your head.* While I understand that world I came from and feel a connection—there's a vast disconnect. Perhaps artists have to live in that world in-between. I've yet to learn how. Neither of my parents finished high school. As a teenager during WWII my father became a member of the Mussolini Youth. My ancestors weren't fascists— in the tiny village outside of Naples people weren't given much of a choice. You gave your boys over. There were consequences. He talked little about his wartime experiences. A story about him in a camp that was a type of prison. One time they attempted to escape and several of his companions were killed. I'm not sure how much of what he told me was true. He and my aunt, his younger sister, remembered bombs going off near their village. My father spoke well of German soldiers. When they occupied the village, he said they were always on their best behavior and treated the villagers with the respect. For all of Mussolini's faults he told me, there were good things like getting the trains to run on time. My father had an older sister who died. He and my surviving aunt said, she died of an illness. The truth is she killed herself. She was given a pistol by my grandmother when she revealed that she had become pregnant. Rumors had it the father might be a German soldier. My grandmother on my father's side is the evilest person I have ever known. I don't doubt for one minute that she forced her daughter to commit such an act. After the war when she left Italy for America, the people in the village had a festival thanking the Virgin Mary to finally be rid of her. My father's older brother came to America with my grandfather before the war. My uncle served in the U.S. Army fighting the Japanese in the Pacific. For the majority of the time when I was growing up, I did not know my uncle. When I was young, he and my father had opened a sandwich shop together and during an argument my uncle spat in my mother's face. My father never forgave him. And they broke contact. My father read the sports page and the racing forms. He loved the horses and dogs. I see him at the breakfast table with a cup of coffee and a cigarette dangling from his mouth, penciling the racing forms. Many years later when I told him I wanted to be a writer he asked me why. I don't remember if I had an answer, or if I did, would he even understand? While he made me go to church, he never attended. When he owned the gas station one of the priests from Saint Francis was a customer. Sometimes he would insist on hearing my father's confession. We were asked to leave the office while the priest sat in a chair and my father knelt down by his side to confess his sins.

9

~

My mother grew up in and around Boston, first generation daughter born of Italian immigrants. Her mother gave birth to eleven children and lost several others during pregnancy. My grandfather on my mother's side was a brutal, hard drinking man who abused his children and beat my grandmother so severely that on different occasions she had to be hospitalized. My grandfather would not allow her out of their home. The son's ran all errands and tended to any business outside the house. It got so bad that this sheltered immigrant who couldn't speak a word of English, gathered up her three youngest daughters and ran away to New York City until several months later one of my uncles located them. My sick grandmother and the three girls had been living in squalor above a baker in the Chelsea section of the city. When she left, I think she feared more for her young daughters than she feared having her husband beat her. My grandmother became so ill the owner of the bakery contacted a neighborhood nurse or social worker of some kind. They were surviving on hot water, and old bread the baker supplied. During her childhood my mother suffered from malnutrition and developed rickets, a softening of the bones due to lack of nutrients. My mother told great stories. Throughout my youth I remember the tales about her childhood. No matter how deep my mother's emotional scars—the storytelling enabled her to transcend them. As painful the content of her stories could be, hope sprouted in the nut of the telling. Her stories were about the power of love and overcoming adversity. She talked at length about the strength of her own mother's love, and no matter how bad things got, she and her siblings always had each other. *It wasn't so bad* she often said. She loved to sing, and sometimes danced. I remember those times where she seemed at her happiest. *Fish gotta swim, birds gotta fly—I'm gonna wash that man right out of my hair—Que serra, serra, whatever will be will be—Moon River, wider than a mile—I'll be down to get you in a taxi honey—*I knew the words to all of those songs. She'd stop her cleaning or cooking, take up her position, smile, and break into song and dance, the kitchen floor, her stage. She gave me the gift of story and song.

~

The old Italians believed in a bit of witchcraft. When I was five or six sick with a bad stomach my mother's mother *sang the worms* to me. My grandmother had been living with us for a brief time. They were readying to put her in a nursing home. The room was dark. I'd been throwing up and crying and my mother came in and told *me grandma's going* to *sing the worms*. I didn't know what she meant. She said Grandma will sing and make the worms in your stomach go away. My mother left my grandmother in the room. She stood over me. I could barely see her gentle face as she began to sing, though it was more of a chant. The pitch of her voice dropped low and swept high all the while she circled her fingertips touching softly around my tummy. It had no healing effect as I recall. But it was eerily unsettling. The old Italian women believed in spells and the evil eye and talismans to ward off offensive energy directed towards them. In the North End there was a very old woman named

Filomena. All the women feared and revered her. She always wore black, and it was said that she could cast spells or break them and tell your fortune. The women spoke in awe when her name was mentioned. In case of a strange occurrence that needed to be dealt with, they whispered amongst themselves, *parliamo con Filomena.*

~

My mother never read books. I remember her paging through picture magazines or the *TV Guide*. She remained dedicated to my father—his needs came first—and the household—dutifully cooking and cleaning, seven days a week. At sixteen she quit school. She told me several times that she'd wanted to be a teacher, but one of my uncle's wives, a hairdresser, talked her into quitting and attending hairdressing school so she could earn a living. I remember my mother in the kitchen cutting the hair of friends and neighborhood women. Until I turned eight or nine, the majority of my down time was spent with my mother and sisters. I have two sisters, Lucille four years older, Betty four years younger. On weekends my mother would take us to visit her relatives. Her brothers and sisters had settled in the Boston area in towns like Revere, West Roxbury, Jamaica Plain and a few farther out into the suburbs. Because my mother had so many siblings, I had lots of aunts, uncles and cousins.

My mother's maiden name was Ferragamo. The Ferragamos were simple people. None of the adults finished high school. One uncle was a barber, another a baker, another drove cab. Like my mother, my aunts stayed home and took care of the houses and children. During the summer my mother took us to the beach—Revere, where my sisters and I begged my mother for a quarter that at the time bought each of us a snack, and a ride on one of the amusements. I loved the Ferris Wheel and cotton candy. Back then Revere Beach was a full amusement park with a legendary roller coaster, food kiosks, arcades and a great boulevard where motorcycles and hot rods cruised the strip. Other days my mother took us to Wrights Pond, a Medford spot for the locals where I ran into kids I knew. There was a food kiosk and I had a taste for their hot dogs. My mother chatted with other moms, poured cold drinks when we thirsted, warned us to take a break from swimming when our lips turned purple and she'd towel us dry.

~

Both my parents knew what it is to starve, each on separate sides of the Atlantic Ocean. When they were old enough and had the means, having a well-stocked kitchen became a priority. On Saturday mornings I accompanied my mother to Boston's North End where she shopped for her meat and produce. We'd take the bus to the old Sullivan Square Station, then board the subway into North Station and walk to the North End. My mother shopped at Tony the Butcher. Tony's was a cramped red storefront with black and white marble floors covered with sawdust. There were scarred, old, wooden meat cutting tables and rabbits and other dead animals hanging outside on hooks. Except for Tony, the butchers spoke Italian. Most of the patrons talked Italian though I think the men in the blood-stained aprons laughed at my mother's bad dialect. Italian not being her first language, relatives teased her for her awkward pronunciations. She bought steaks, chops, chickens, lamb, veal, sausages, rabbits and whatever else Tony might have special that week. Our purchases wrapped in paper then packed in heavy paper bags, I would carry them back through the streets to North Station where we'd ride the train to Sullivan Square then onto the bus and our walk home from the bus stop. My mother planned the menu for the week. Some of the meat went into the freezer and some to the refrigerator. She cooked a full meal every night and I learned how to prepare veal cutlets that she breaded, fried and baked in the oven topped with tomato sauce and cheese. Sometimes she roasted a whole chicken—sometimes she cut the chicken into pieces and baked it with roasted potatoes, garlic, and mushrooms topped with a pinch of oregano and some grated Romano cheese. When I went to Italy as an adult, my cousin prepared chicken the same way. She learned how to cook everything the way my father wanted, the recipes that he grew up with. One of my favorite dishes was pork chops with fried vinegar peppers and potatoes. On Friday nights we always ate fish, haddock topped with chopped tomatoes, parsley and a little garlic or shrimp in a tomato sauce served over linguine. Every Saturday night we ate steak though occasionally she would she would roast pork or lamb with oven-roasted potatoes. On Sundays was the big gravy with meatballs, sausages and braciolas after pasta. Braciolas are flattened meat—

chicken, pork, beef or veal sprinkled with herbs and cheese and pine nuts and dried fruit or pieces of hardboiled eggs—could be anything—then the meat is rolled up and tied off and seared in a pan before simmering in the gravy. We lived to eat. During the week I walked briskly home from school, my mouth watering for a meatball which she would already have fried, or a small cutlet that she had put aside for me, or a slice of Italian bread topped with a simmering tomato sauce. I spent yards of time in the kitchen with her—mixing meatballs, straining tomatoes for the gravy, putting my thumb on the thread to hold it as she rolled the braciolas, cutting vegetables or peeling potatoes. Cooking became a passion—and remains so to this day.

~

During those pre-gas station years, I had the most free time ever in my childhood. There were chores for me to do at home: bring out the trash, mow the lawn, rake the leaves, shovel snow, feed the dogs and clean their pen. My father happened to be an avid rabbit hunter and kept beagles in a pen that he built on an out-of-the-way side of the house. I planned my chores around the fun to be had. The baby-boomer babies came to fruition in the 1960s. Across Medford, the working and lower-middle class families blossomed. First generation Irish seemed to have the largest families—on Park Street there were the Moynihans with twelve and the Sullivans with ten. Three kids were rare two even rarer. Four and five children were not uncommon, and on every street corner or public park there were plenty of kids to hang out with—to play sports as the season's changed, take a hike to Wright's Pond to swim or fish, get on your bike and ride out to Malden or Somerville or Arlington. I got to know all the families on the street and call on kids or they'd call on me and knew my parents like I knew their parents and where are you going and what time we'll be back. There were mostly Italian and Irish on Park Street. The Irish people I knew—besides having more kids—ate differently from us. Food being such an integral part of our life, that stood out. Irish families appeared to focus less on meals. They ate things like hot dogs and beans, peanut butter and jelly sandwiches, and drank a lot of milk. They weren't as likely to eat together. There'd be some supper on the stove for whomever seemed to be around and hungry. Italian men were fond of gambling, the Irish dads were happier drinking. Those days were possibly the most enjoyable and peaceful of my childhood. The shroud of family problems and real life had not yet descended. What pure joy to fall off to sleep staring at a new pair of Keds high-top sneakers on the floor by my bed, eager to wake the next day, round up the local kids and head to the park for baseball or to throw a football or some kind of kid shenanigans.

~

Eventually my father realized the potential of free labor, and how to keep me under his watchful eye. He began taking me to work with him. The gas station I wrote about in my novel is the one I remember. That place introduced me to the outside world. I learned about business and politics and people. I knew priests, police, crooked police, politicians, businessmen, teachers, carpenters, bookies, drunks, bikers, veterans of various wars, plumbers, truck drivers even prostitutes. In my pocket at the age of fourteen, I carried what was known as the gas roll—essentially the working capital of the day. It could be as little as fifty or as many as several hundred dollars. This was before credit and debit cards. Business transactions were cash, or occasionally check. I met amazing mechanics. Men that could build a drag racing car or roadster from scratch. They were the first real artists I knew. I sat with them on cold cement floors taking engines apart and putting it all back together until it turned over and hummed. Later in life, when I discovered Herman Melville, I became fascinated by the encyclopedic way he wrote about ships. In his exhaustive descriptions of ship tasks, the intricacies of rope knots or the sweeping range of characters that could inhabit one place—I find the universals in the particulars. Rebuilding an engine with the mechanics as it hung on a hook chained to a block and tackle in that damp, cavernous garage—we were the whalers on the ship's deck, surrounding the hanging carcass readying to *cut in*. Theirs the age of the whale. Mine the age of the automobile. For many years I worked right through vacations and after school and weekends during the school year. In summertime it was six or seven days a week—seven in the morning to five at night or sometimes until nine closing. My father picked me up after school, we'd go directly to the station and I'd work until five or sometimes nine. I worked Saturdays and occasionally Sundays. To be fair, I did have a car as soon as I was old enough. I got free gas and when I needed spending cash, he gave it to me. But for me, it came down to having a choice. If I had my mine, I would have done it differently. Not that I could have voiced my opinion back then. I could not go against him—not for anything. I think it's where my attraction to anti-authority comes from. From the early rock and rollers and other cultural icons to authors like Thoreau, Kerouac, to Taoists recluses who left society to live in mountain huts, to the anarchists. Those times that my father struck me or woke me at first light to work a fourteen-hour day leaving me no say in the matter—there the roots of my anarchism. The political is personal.

~

My mother's oldest brother played violin. Uncle Louie lived the better part of his adult life committed in the old State Hospital in Mattapan and later Danvers. Each aunt or uncle had their own version about what happened to Louie. He became family myth. Apparently, he suffered mental breakdowns and ultimately, could not function in the real world. My grandfather, normally a tyrant, favored his oldest son Louie as a child and went so far as to pay for music lessons. When the teachers from the music school came to the house to talk with my grandfather, they told him that my uncle had a special talent, and they offered some kind of scholarship to send him to the conservatory. I never asked what anyone meant by conservatory or what special school my uncle Louie attended. Even my mother, a woman with a limited vocabulary, used that word conservatory. I never met Uncle Louie. He died when I was five or six. My parents spoke of visiting him. They would bring food that my mother prepared. He'd eat slowly. It seemed like he recognized her. But he didn't talk. Sometimes he would look at her and grunt. He took a lot of medicine she told me and slept most of the time. Music is my first love. My father had Perry Como records, and cha-cha records and I listened obsessively to a single called "Sleepwalk" by Santo and Johnny, a steel guitar and guitar instrumental—such expression of feeling went right through me. My father and mother liked to dance. The only time I remember them happy together they were dancing. But you can't dance every day. My father kept those singles in a blue record box with a handle and lid. The record player had built-in speaker and the mono sound spewed out Latin beats and love ballads. I heard Chuck Berry and Eddie Cochran at the gas station when the mechanics listened to their transistor radios, and on Friday nights they gathered and played rock and roll at one of their apartments. They had electric guitars and small amps and the drummer might set up a high-hat and snare. When I had the honor of an invitation, I marveled at how much fun they had, the amount of beer they drank and how they could feel and play this music. They were the archetypal '50s guys with slicked-back haircuts, tattoos and a pack of Lucky Strikes or Camels rolled up in their white t-shirt sleeves. When they struck up a backbeat, they travelled to another realm, and took me with them. My parents pushed the accordion on me. It's an Italian thing. After seeing the Beatles on *The Ed Sullivan Show* I wanted an electric guitar. Rock and roll can and continues to radicalize people. It did me. When I saw how outraged my father became that first night that we watched the Beatles on Ed Sullivan, I knew there was something in rock and roll for me. They incensed him. He hated the music. He hated their long hair. *They should spend some time in jail and smarten up. They have no respect for anyone.* I wanted what they had. My parents brought me down the street to Pampalone Music School. The place was right out of a Lenny Bruce bit. I insisted on guitar lessons and they talked me into trying the accordion first. I reluctantly took a rental accordion home, made a few half-hearted attempts and put my foot down: electric guitar. I don't know how, but I got my way. I'll never forget that avocado green, Danelectro single-pickup guitar and the tiny practice amplifier. Rentals. Problem was the school enrolled me in the Mel Banks guitar system where you bought the Mel Banks books as you went along and learned how to read and play music. But I wanted to play rock and roll of which, my fifty-or-so-year-old teacher, and the Mel Banks books seemed to know nothing about. I never did learn how to rock and roll at Pampalone's. But something I never dreamed of occurred during the course of my lessons there. All music schools have an annual recital. Parents pay good money for lessons and instrument rentals and want to see the fruits of their investments. The night of the recital we marched out on the stage, one by one, the good, the bad, and the oblivious. Accordionists. Drummers. Pianists. Guitarists. I played a stiff melody of "Spanish Eyes" while my teacher Mr. Piciarello accompanied me on rhythm. It was a song that my father loved, and he'd asked Mr. Piciarello to teach it to me. At the end of the student performances, the teachers played. I never heard jazz before. Perhaps I had inkling from bad television stereotypes. But there they were, four nerdish, Italian American men on fire in the auditorium of the Roberts Junior High School. I know not what they played but that they played like their lives depended on it. Fat, bald Mr. D'Orvidio plucked up and down the bass so intensely sweat from his forehead flew around him. Mr. Piciarello worked his guitar as if it were another limb. Guy, we got to call him by his first name because he was younger than the other three teachers, played vibes and Mr. Meloni played drums—how delicate he handled the sticks he seemed to have magic wrists. I didn't know what was happening. I didn't understand what this meant but I knew for sure these four men were in another space and time. It would be years before I finally *got* it and jazz wash over me like a rough surf over a toddler.

~

The gas station was a nexus for storytellers. So many different people I'd be in contact with each day, so many stories. The mechanics continually told tales of their pasts—one had been in the military and stationed abroad, one had ridden with motorcycle gangs, another a drag racer at the Epping Speedway on Sundays. They never stopped talking about girls and sex and bragged and teased each other. Some were married others lived with their parents but whenever a group of them gathered around the station, they spun yarns. One day there was a fire at the gas station and in no time, it became the stuff of local myth. One of the mechanics working for my father happened to be an area legend. He'd come with a reputation of being a little crazy, teller of fibs, and not nearly the mechanic that he deemed himself to be. He'd once worked on a crew for a well-known drag racer. He claimed he was a mechanic but we all knew he was a gofer—he was the one who would go for coffee, or pick up parts and wash cars. After a few weeks working at the station, it became clear that all of these things I'd heard about him were true—he was mostly talk. One evening while gassing up a car he was smoking at the pumps and somehow a hot ash fell on some spilled gas and the car caught on fire. He was able to warn the driver to get out and shut the emergency switch off in time, but the car burned, and the pumps were damaged. The story got written up in the local paper and they interviewed the mechanic. Johnny Barnes was his name, and he told his story of the entire event. As the days wore on and he continued telling it to different people it changed in small increments until it became something else. The final story that he told was not the way it happened but the things he changed seemed to make the facts more enticing. He grew excited and heroic as he reported the event—until people stopped asking him and the fire slipped into our collective memory. My father used to buy our work shoes at a store in nearby Malden Square. It was located on the second floor of an old redbrick factory building. A woman and her husband owned the store. Wherever we went during the course of the day, the parts store, the sub shop, the coffee shop, or the transmission specialists— there was always time for a short visit—some banter and gossip—someone had a story. At that time there had been a great fire. Half of Malden

Square burned down. Somehow the shoe store building was spared, and several weeks later my dad took me to buy new work shoes. The woman told us about the fire, where it began and what started it, how it burned block-by-block, building by building, closer to them. I imagined she'd been changing her story like Johnny Barnes. She finished the story with the words *finally, the firemen came up and told us to leave the building. Finally, the firemen came up and told us to leave the building.* For days I kept repeating those words, turning them over in my head, recalling the woman telling her tale. She'd been telling it for weeks I imagined, and unbeknownst to me at the time, she'd made poetry. Her rhythms and rhymes got under my skin like the backbeat of a Beatles song. The firemen came up and told us to leave the building.

~

Kerouac is my door. I didn't read *On the Road* first, but *The Town and the City*, probably Kerouac's most conventional book. The long, loving descriptions of Lowell, the mills, the river, immigrant neighborhoods and the working-class life were brought over in a narrative that sang a new song to me. Up to that point, I didn't think this kind of writing could be literature. Literature, I thought, had to be by and about other people—not of my class or my experiences—of the *literati*—though I didn't know that word yet. I'd been yearning for what I didn't know, and I grew excited with Kerouac's writing about New York and how it changed him forever. Leaving the town behind, in a way he'd betrayed his past while in new circles of people he often felt like a stranger. I identified with the fictional Martin family—especially the eldest son Joe Martin and the father George who like my father was an immigrant, ran his own business and gambled. When I finished that book, a light had come on. Kerouac led me to the Beats, the writers of the San Francisco Renaissance, New York School, and Black Mountain. I was never the same after that.

I felt as if I'd been given the permission to live freely, even if it went against everything I'd been taught. This all came about as other circumstances in my life were shifting such as new love and friendships and immersing myself in punk rock—all of it pushing me in a new direction. Reading the Beats, I followed their queues. I began devouring books—novels, philosophy, poetry, science and history—in no organized way. I had no system. I felt that any good book, or for that matter movie, painting, score of music, held a piece of an incomplete puzzle. In a matter of a few years I had affairs with Charles Ives, Duke Ellington and Mingus, Emma Goldman, Pollock, Picasso. Kubrick, Wells, Fellini, Bach, Cezanne, Bird, Monk, Blake, Copland, Whitman, Sappho, Dickens, Parker, Miles, Woolf, Dickinson, Stein, Pound, Li Po, Tu Fu, Taoism, Buddhism, Confucius, so much more. One thing just led to another. I frequented new and used bookstores and record stores, museums, art galleries, punk shows, jazz bars and poetry readings. They were everywhere back then. I couldn't get enough. I felt that the more I could take on and discover, the closer I would get to this unidentifiable place where everything might be right. The closer I got, the farther away I grew from where I came from, though later I learned that there is no ideal space. I've never felt I belong in the artist's world, and I can't go back to where I came from.

~

No matter how far I have traveled as a reader, with the exception of the Chinese, American writing has it all for me. It's about the vernacular—the pitch, fall and turns of the local—Lorine Niedecker's *weedy speech*. I hear it in our slave narratives, I've always been drawn to them, where learning to read and write means empowerment, freedom and liberation. It's that American twang I hear in the syntax of Mark Twain, Whitman, Melville, Stein, Williams, Hughes, Kerouac to name a few. Some of his methodology aside, Eliot never connected with me. Neither did Henry James or Robert Lowell. Faulkner did for sure, mostly in his technique and *Sound and the Fury* stood above them all. Hemingway some—the short stories. I've never been a big fan of the novels. I don't know what it is, but I can smell it. America. There's an interview with William Carlos Williams where he talks about how we speak American not English, and writers would do well to remember that. I'm not making a quality judgment on any of the authors I name. Taste is all. I go by my ear.

~

I suppose the American thing is where jazz fits in. Rooted in Africa and the slave experience, it's America's greatest artistic contribution to the world. It's the *feeling* in jazz that hooked me— the emotion swirling in those sounds and rhythms—the joy, sadness, love, lament, and humor—the stuff of life. And as importantly—the spontaneity and improvisatory quality—a going-on-your-nerve—poet Charles Olson's one thing leading onto the next, the approach the abstract expressionist painters took. Kerouac's prose would be nothing without that jazz understructure—the sense of risk, the acceptance of failure, the rhythms and rhymes of words placed together. Kerouac didn't learn to speak English until he was four. His parents spoke French Canadian. During his boyhood in Lowell there were Germans, Greeks, Italians, Poles as well as French Canadians among others. Kerouac grew up hearing numerous languages floating on the air. At the same time, English was a relative term. Some spoke it well, others learned it bit by bit, and you couldn't exhaust various versions of English spoken in that city. A good ear hears these things, stores these things, even if not consciously. If you don't speak the language—the sound's all around. When I wrote *Gas Station* I kept in mind Jack Kerouac's *Dr. Sax.* Whenever I would find myself unsure or faltering, I turned to the opening paragraph in Kerouac's book—the boy narrator describes a dream where he is sitting on the sidewalk in his hometown of Lowell, Massachusetts, pencil and paper in hand, trying to describe the world around him. He tells himself not to stop and think of the words, and if he does stop, just stop *to think of the picture better—and let your mind off yourself.* The eye by way of the ear.

~

As a boy, sports appealed to me. I played some hockey and baseball. Threw a football around. Never had any instincts on a basketball court. I liked watching sports on television. Mostly baseball and hockey. The Red Sox were never a great team. Carl Yastrzemski as good as it got. I did manage to see Bobby Orr and the Big Bad Bruins play at the Boston Garden. My father loved hockey, and he would get cheap seats way up in the heavens and take me once in a while. But I had no natural proclivity for playing sports. They put me in right field in little league baseball. I'd stand out there in my own little world watching butterflies and hoping that nobody hit the ball to me. But for boys there seemed to be no escape from sports. We were expected to play. We were expected to be sports fans. Those that excelled in sports were held in higher esteem than others. I didn't fantasize about being a major league pitcher. I dreamed about playing in a band and having people screaming in the audience. Music made me feel alive. Even as a writer, the works of mine that I feel best about are the ones where the language dances. My oldest sister took tap dancing lessons. I watched her rehearse at home, tapping along on the kitchen floor to records playing. Sometimes I sat at the dancing school and watched the classes—fascinated by the music and the clacking taps marking out a rhythm as the body swayed. Most of the tap students were girls but there were one or two boys interspersed amongst them. There were dance recitals where the kids performed ballet, tap, jazz. My sister wore a fancy costume and make up and our entire family sat in the audience. I remember one particular family who were highly admired at the school. There were two sisters, and a brother. They were the top students and the two sisters got to dance together, and the boy did a tap dance alone. Even their father was a dancer and performed with the daughters during one song. They were so good they could be on television. At least I thought. For a while I got it into my head that I wanted to take up tap dancing. My sister laughed at me and said I'd never be able to learn. My parents discouraged me from the first time I brought it up. But I kept pressing and began practicing at home without tap shoes. I'd learned some basic things from watching my sister like the shuffle ball chain and for what must have been several months I did not let up. My father was most adamantly against it. *That's not for boys* he argued. *Why would you want to do that?* Eventually something gave, and my parents took me down to talk with the dance teacher. Little did I know at the time that they all had been scheming behind my back. The teacher told me that my feet were too small, and I wouldn't be able to learn the steps and adapt to the shoes correctly. I was young, still prepubescent. The girls' feet were smaller than mine. But girls are different they insisted. Maybe in a year. I had no choice but to go along with it. Eventually, my dancing ambitions waned. But my ears still perk up when I hear the sound of foot taps on a hard floor.

~

My love for history led me to write *The Bystander's Scrapbook*. History is malleable and subjective. In books, movies, literature, documentaries, and television, history plays itself out in a continual barrage of half-truths, hearsay, falsifications, suppositions, and revisions. The material for the historian is made up of letters, documents, records, personal accounts, journals, diaries, and archeological evidence to name a few. Sometime in my thirties I met a man who would become a lifelong friend and mentor. He was old enough to be my father. Bob D'Attillio and I met at a poetry gathering. A group of poets and I were meeting weekly at my apartment, reading Dante's *Divine Comedy* aloud in the original Italian. Bob came with a mutual poet friend. We began talking about jazz and both shared a love for it. Later we met for coffee. A lifelong Medford resident, Bob was a historian and anarchist who had dedicated his life to the study of the Sacco and Vanzetti case. Through my relationship with Bob, I learned about anarchism which became an obsession and brought me back into the history of my Italian American roots, beyond Sacco and Vanzetti I discovered Errico Malatesta, Gramsci, Garibaldi, Arturo Giovannitti—the man that tried to blow up Attorney General Palmer during the Palmer Raids after World War I. What a great surprise to learn that nearly hundred years before me, Giovannitti had lived in Somerville, not more than a few blocks away from where I have lived more than half of my life. History can catch you that way. Anarchism is an easy sell for me. *The least amount of authority possible.* If you knew my father, you'd understand. After several years researching the subject, I felt as if I had a mass of information that I wanted to do something with. Dos Passos's *U.S.A Trilogy* had left an impression. And the collaged books of Paul Metcalf were a revelation. Collage became the method. *The Bystander's Scrapbook* is a collage—fragments of documents, narrative, newspaper articles, journals, diary entries—some real, some made up. Bob told me you can't write a historical novel and make things up. For me the best part of being a writer has always been that I can do anything that I want. Of all the novels I wrote that could scare an audience away. Run far, run fast—it is *The Bystander's Scrapbook.* I still can't believe that I found a publisher. Probably my worst selling novel—and that's really saying something. But I remain very proud of that book.

~

I don't have a Bible now, but I have numerous editions of the *Tao Te Ching*, the *Lieh-Tzu* and the *Chuang Tzu*—the three essential texts in philosophical Taoism—not to be confused with religious Taoism whose rituals and beliefs would make the Catholics look like Universalists though the two types of Taoism do overlap. Through Kerouac and the Beats, I discovered Buddhism. For a while I fancied myself a Buddhist. I learned to meditate, went vegetarian, I even bought a wool coat made in Tibet. I learned about the various types of Buddhism, especially drawn to the ideas of Zen. I read the Sutras and tried to see life through the eyes of a Buddhist. I devoured Alan Watts and the poetry of Gary Snyder. I used to meditate naked. I went thru a phase where nudity held some kind of persuasion over me. But certain tenets about Buddhism did not settle well. True, it didn't have the typical crap of the monotheistic Western religions—yet the basic message told me that there was something fundamentally wrong with me as a human, and I could change that if I acted and lived a certain way. At least that's how I heard it. One morning while meditating naked I felt a fart come on and lifted a cheek slightly to release it when a spot of shit about the size of a quarter popped out on the living room carpet in the apartment I shared with Molly. I took it as a sign that Buddhism was not for me. Taoism had no such baggage. It finally sunk into me that if someone names a god, or truth, or real Tao— well, they're full of shit. Like anarchism, Taoism was a good fit for me. *Nothing* is way better than *Something*.

~

Before I ever took a drink, or smoked a cigarette, or experienced drugs, I was attracted to all of the above. As a child I pretended to smoke and drink and couldn't wait until I was old enough. My parents held parties and gatherings and all their friends smoked and drank and when they had a few drinks in them they changed. They grew silly, let their guards down, had fun. I removed the cigarette butts from my father's ashtrays and smoked them. I gagged and coughed and nearly puked—but it made me dizzy and I liked it. I fantasized about drinking and would sneak sips from the bottom of drink and beer glasses after my parents had a party. Then I became fascinated with marijuana which I'd been hearing about. The Beatles were using it after all. It couldn't be that bad. I used to pretend sick a lot as a youngster so I could stay home from school. One day when my mother was gone, maybe she was working part time then, or had to be somewhere long enough, I drank shots of whiskey from the liquor closet. I'd never known such warmth and safety. I fell asleep on the sofa and woke to my mother's hands shaking me. She must not have smelled it on my breath—surely it had to have been there—and all I could think of was how I wanted more—to do it again. I couldn't have been older than eleven or twelve. But that warm, soft feeling in my stomach and the emotional release it brought seduced me like a toy store. This would be the beginning of a long relationship.

~

The first time I ever attempted to write, at least in some kind of creative way, I must have been ten or so. I had never been exposed to any kind of reading, except for the old SRA we had at school. SRA was a reading and comprehension program where students read fiction, non-fiction articles and stories then responded to multiple choice questions. As they progressed, students advanced to numerous color-coded levels. I do remember in third grade reading my way up through the colors. We were allowed to read from the SRA during down time, when we had finished an in-class assignment, or sometimes on a Friday afternoon the last hour or two of class when the teacher must have been burned-out and needed a break. I worked my way through those colors and up the ladder. Once finished with a story, I had to show the teacher who would allow me on to the next story in that color. Upon finishing all the stories in that color, you moved up to the next color, and the reading and questions were more demanding. I got obsessed with it and never being much of a promising student, my third-grade teacher Miss De Gregorio seemed surprised at the urgency with which I approached the SRA, and my quick success. I had no idea what it meant. But I read my way to the top and finished the entire series before the school year finished. Why did I became so enthralled with those stories? I don't remember even one now. But some point a year or two later I had a blank notebook at home. How it came into my hands I can't recall. I got the urge to write and wrote a story about a young boy who had a '57 Chevy in his driveway and spent all of his spare time tinkering with it. Mornings before school, after school, weekends, he could be found in the driveway, toolbox open, working away— starting the engine, sitting in the car and driving it up and down the driveway. I only recently remembered that story, though the memory of thinking about the process of writing, as I look back and reflect, is vivid. I knew during that act, that I was writing a story. I had no fundamental idea of writing at all. Or what drove me to do it. But I knew there were books. The library was filled with them. I knew that people wrote those books, and they were called authors. I knew no one who read books. Looking at the stacks of them put me in awe. To what purpose did they serve? For the longest time I didn't know how to use a library. Probably in school I'd been taught the card catalog system—but there were letters and decimal points and I could never figure it out. It wasn't until college it came together—and the library opened up into the world.

~

1965. Fifth grade. Ten years old. By then the potential slog of everyday life had begun saturating
my consciousness. I felt it strongest at school.
Fifth grade was my worst school year yet. My
misbehaving antics increased with problems at
home, and my father's acting out. My father was
seeing the mother of a girl in my class. The girl
used to tell me at school, your father was at our
house yesterday, or last night. One day my
mother drove over to the address, walked in, and
bagged him sitting at the kitchen table over a cup
of coffee. It began a long, difficult time of their
fighting, my father leaving home for a while,
moving back in. They'd always fought. Even before then. Like driving back to Medford after a
visit to relatives in the North End and my father
threatening to drive off the road and kill us all.
Or my father yelling and throwing a pot of spa-
ghetti on the kitchen wall and my mother dutifully cleaning it up. I acted out at school. I had
trouble remaining in my seat. I passed notes.

Performed silly antics for the students around me. I developed a passion for shooting spitballs. I was taking guitar lessons by then, and the teacher had to call my parents when I disrupted the band practice. Or I was thrown out of Boy Scouts for helping to tie a kid up with ropes and lock him in the big wooden rope box. But school became my greatest disappointment. Having to sit in one room for six and a half hours per day and be force fed math, history, geography, science, reading and writing felt like slavery. School seemed so wasteful and unrewarding. The kids that dutifully went through the paces to do what was expected were dull and uninteresting. Then in fifth grade a gift I never imagined, I had to have my appendix removed. Back then you were allowed much more time to heal. It got me out of school for three weeks. The *Rubber Soul* album had just been released. Those three weeks were the first big turning point in my life. I played the grooves of that album, over and over, every day. While I had already been crazy about the Beatles, this record was an epiphany. The songs more serious than anything of theirs in the past. They seemed to be about life. As if the Beatles knew how I had been thinking and feeling. I pantomimed and faked played and sang along. "I'm Looking Through You," "Think for Yourself," "In My Life." I fell in love with the idea that I might not have to do what everybody else did for my entire life. There were people out there who got to do what they wanted to do. John, Paul, George and Ringo did not get up every day and have to go to dull jobs. They got up and played music. Created. Like so many things back then I didn't understand what it meant to create. But inside me I sensed something. I burned. I longed. I thought, maybe there could be another way. At ten years old those three weeks away from the daily grind awakened in me a newfound hope and passion for possibilities in life. I didn't have to be a *nowhere man*. I could *think for myself.*

~

None of my aunts and uncles spoke proper English. In fact, most folks I grew up around didn't. My father's hybrid vernacular was a cross between peasant southern Italian dialect, and broken English. My mother spoke in fragments. Her sentences short incomplete bursts. She had a habit of prefacing her statements with *they say*. My sisters and I would tease her—who's *they* Ma? She'd grow flustered. After decades of hearing my mother's stories about her childhood, I decided to use it as material for my novel, *They Say*. The narrative is made up of five first-person narratives, and one third-person narrative. The first-person narratives were taken from my uncles' and my aunts' speech patterns and stories. Each had unique voices and idioms. Five siblings tell the story of their family, especially a brother, an artist, who went mad and had to be hospitalized for the rest of his life. The third person narrative focuses on the life of that brother through an omniscient point of view. For four of the siblings' voices I boiled down elements of my many aunts and uncles, but for the fifth, I used my mother's manner of talking, as close as I could get it, and based that sister's character specifically on her. Through abject poverty, physical and emotional abuse, the story of the Pellegrino family unravels. Amongst this uneducated family, none of whom had any real sense of art or where it fit in to their gruesome lives, this child prodigy, my uncle Louie in real life, emerged. While I have no idea the diagnosis of my uncle's mental illness, my sense is manic depression. It seems he had bouts of mania interspersed with long, deep depression. Later in my life when I was diagnosed with a bipolar disorder, I wondered if the source of the genetic roots could be traced to my mother's family. How could a dark, emotionally persecuted person, so different from everyone else in this world of deprivation and ignorance, come into being?

Italian-American Literature and Working-Class Culture 421

is an immigrant saga from a very different perspective. The Pelligrinos are not the usual lovely, honorable, happy urban family, whose trials and tribulations in poverty are overcome to lead them all to the promised land of the suburbs and middle-class bliss. Torra's writing has a freshness that is rare in today's world of fiction. He is not afraid to take chances or to make his reader work. The reader needs to get used to reading "they say" and it takes more than just a few pages. First of all, "they" are all the brothers and sisters of Louie, who is trapped in a working-class immigrant family that can handle his talent but not his eccentricities. Second, most of them speak in a vocabulary and style that has not left elementary school, and so one finds oneself mouthing the words out loud in order to follow the normal non-sequiturs that happen when people speak. Only when we access Louie's perspective does the language shift to standard English, a strange occurrence because, according to the other characters, Louie is the one who is crazy. There is no punctuation and no chapters, so readers must pay close attention when one voice begins and another ends. There are very subtle

~

I smoked pot several times before I realized its effects. Winter, I was fifteen. An older friend had a car and several of us had gone sledding at a golf course in nearby Stoneham. When we arrived and parked the car, we smoked several bowls. I felt nothing at first and figured it would be a dead end like my other early attempts. We unloaded our sleds from the trunk and made our way to the crest of the hill. Upon arriving, I ran with my sled in hands, then tossed it onto the ground with myself on top and flew down the steep side of the hill. At the bottom, I rose and proceeded to drag my sled up. Suddenly something swept over me like wave from the bottom of the sea rising up then crashing down. I could hear a vibrating whoosh inside my ears. It repeated and repeated again. This is what the kids must have been referring to when they used the term a *rush*. Mind and body transferred to another world. I felt tingly, happy, warm. My thought patterns became elastic. Everything looked different. At the top of the hill I quickly swished back down, huge smile on my face, mouth open, snow scraps dusting my face. Each time I made my way back up the hill, the rushes began again. What delights waited inside me to be born? The drive home was a combination of profound insights and absurdities. Music blared on the radio. It never sounded this way before. I laughed hysterically, and on the next breath grew serious and concerned about the most minute thought. When I got home, I had a voracious appetite. I ate a bowl of leftover lasagna. A chicken leg. Meatballs. Boy are you hungry today my mother commented. Like the time I took my first drink—I wanted more.

~

There were no fine artists where I came from. Only Uncle Louie, but he went insane. I remember graduating high school, and a certain group of the kids at school were applying for college. But they were mostly Jewish kids. I knew some of them peripherally at school, but none were close friends. I hung with the working-class Italians and Irish. In home room the college bound kids shared notes, and talked about which schools they might attend, what they might study when they got there. But for the Italian kids, the Irish kids, the future was toil. Some were going into trades. One of my friends would work in his father's garment factory in Boston. Another would go from part-time to full-time in his father's sub and pizza shop. Others were hoping to get hired by the city to throw trash on garbage trucks, or work for the post office, or apprentices to tradesmen. My father had recently sold his gas station for a secure job working in a state garage. I'd played music in some bands and that was my fantasy. There were a handful of kids from the city who were notable musicians, they had aspirations to continue their pursuits. My mother always wanted me to work in a bank. *Why don't you go down the square to the Medford Savings Bank*? After high school I bounced around for years, worked retail, short order cook, painted houses, loading docks, turned wrenches in a garage. Playing music drifted farther away. But eventually I took up reading. I read on my lunch hour or on my coffee breaks. Bookman, that's what the mechanics called me—one of them fond of saying that he hated book smart people. That was something I heard said often where I came from. One day I told an old corner friend that I wanted to be a writer. He looked at me as if I'd grown a third eye and asked: *Who the fuck do you think you are?*

~

I smoked my first full cigarette with Patty. Before that it had been butts from my father's ashtrays. We were behind the Curtis School—the Schoolyard we called it. A group of us hung out there. Sometimes we tossed a football around. Or we *hit them out*—a batter tossing a baseball up and hitting to others in the field waiting with gloves. But mostly we sat around on the concrete steps and talked. We tried to talk like grownups. Swore a lot. Spit. Tomboy is what they called girls like Patty. She had curly short hair, freckles and thick eyeglasses. She hit, caught and threw the ball better than any of the boys—the only female in the group. It was a Winston, and she lit if for me. As we smoked, she explained things about women's vaginas to me. How they worked. How women got sexual pleasure. Very matter of fact. I grew embarrassed. I'm not sure how we got onto it—perhaps I'd asked her a question of some kind—it's very complicated down there she said. I'd never known a lesbian before. I don't think we called it that then. She didn't hide it. I like boys for some things she told me, but for other things I like girls. She must have been

57

fourteen at the time. Me a year younger. There were already rumors about her brother Tommy. He never played sports and smoked Salem menthols and seemed to be more like a girl than a boy. Their older brother Johnny had a reputation in the neighborhood as a tough guy. He'd spent time in reform school for breaking into houses and selling stolen goods to Nate down at Nate's Spa. Nate was a big fat guy who chewed on stubby cigars and invited us to the back room where he kept gay porn. Tommy often hung out at Nate's Spa with a group of like boys. Nobody really cared about all that stuff at the time. We gossiped a bit, but Tommy and Patty were as welcome around as any kid. Years later I began a novel about what happened to Patty. Sometimes storylines are handed to you. Triple murder suicide. Didn't get any better than that. But every time I tried to write about it, I failed. I'd get ten or twenty or once, fifty pages into it and things would fall apart. It took a long time before I wrote the third, and title novel of the *My Ground Trilogy*. My past efforts, I realized, had been about me. I was the center of the writing. She was a friend who'd suffered—let's say a tragic fate—and my writing focused on how it affected me—like a badge of honor—look at this kid and what he experienced as a boy. Eventually, I got hip to the fact that the book was not about me. It had nothing to do with me and so I removed my character from the book entirely. After that, like all my fiction, the book seemed to write itself. It's the bleakest book I've ever penned. I wrote in a very bad emotional state—a deep depression and desperation wicked as I have ever experienced. Most of the writing occurred in the middle of the night—insomnia has been a lifelong problem. I wrote in the dark, no lights except for the computer screen. On the desk one side of me an old-fashioned espresso pot, on the other side a bong. Upon finishing I suffered a severe crash that took weeks from which to recover. But I'd finally gone back for Patty, of all people, I couldn't leave her behind.

MY GROUND
By Joseph Torra
Weidenfeld & Nicolson, £6.99
ISBN 0 575 06849 3

☎ £5.99 (free p&p) 0870 160 8080
IN A suburb of Massachusetts, the 40-year-old amnesiac Lauren Bell sits in her flat trying to piece together the memories of her life. She remembers childhood escapades, sexual encounters and hospital wards. But, as the truth emerges, it appears that her past is best forgotten. Torra's evocation of his narrator's twisted white-trash milieu is brilliantly done, creating an uneasy portrait of life on the fringes of sanity and society.
Jerome Boyd Maunsell

~

By my late teens my obsession with getting high was in full tilt. My mid-teens to early twenties, most of my spare time found me with my friends in search of drugs. As we grew older booze became readily available. But it was not enough. We took acid, mescaline, speed, barbiturates, pot and angel dust. We'd drive around Medford, from one corner or park to the next, to find out who was selling what where. If that failed, we drove to Malden High School. For years, dozens and dozens of kids lined up in front of Malden High, while carloads of kids pulled up to purchase the drug de jour. If we could not find drugs, we bought Dramamine motion sickness pills at the drug store. We'd devour an entire pack each, can't remember how many in a pack— but the result led to a total thrashing of the senses and hallucinations. I don't know how I snuck it all by my parents, though they were clueless about those things then. The only worry I ever had was that they might smell alcohol on my breath. I spent countless nights wide awake in my bed high on speed, or watching my walls melt, swell and deflate while tripping on acid. I sat at the dinner table high on acid watching a steak move around on my plate. In the morning I rose and went to school, or later, after my father sold the gas station, to my job. On a weekend day I'd meet up with friends and get high all over again. By the time I was in my mid-twenties, while not physically addicted to one specific drug, I was completely dependent on substances, and it became hard to imagine any day without some kind of buzz.

~

I started using substances to save my life. I stopped using them to save my life. My teen years were desperate. I had no control over anything. If not in school, you could find me working at my father's gas station or doing chores at home. He kept me busy, my father—and used me like property. Take out the trash, mow the lawn, rake the leaves, shovel the snow, mow the neighbor's lawns, shovel their walks, take out their trash. I had so little time for myself. At any moment, my father could find a reason to blow up at me—then I'd be in for verbal and/or physical abuse. If I said something he didn't like at the dinner table, he would swipe me across the face with a backhander. He could kick, smack or punch, but his weapon of choice—his belt. He'd take it off, strap me where I stood, I'd fall onto the floor, roll myself up into a ball, protect my face and upper body so he'd go after my legs, leaving welts on my thighs that smarted for days. I hated him. I wished secretly that he would die.

I dreamed of a day when I would be older, and he would have no power over me. It was no wonder when I had a free afternoon or evening and I began to drink, or smoke pot, or take a little pill—and found myself *feeling ok*—that I ran with it. Who wouldn't? It was mine, and only mine, and I controlled it and when high, he had no control over me. Call it escape. Call it self-medication. Call it survival. Call it control. Or all of the above. As the years passed it didn't stop. I became dependent on using for everything, especially later with writing. Much of my poetry, and most of my novels, were written under the influence of pot, and often with a hangover on board. As the years went on one of my excuses for not stopping was the fear of not being able to create. Approaching forty, I remember thinking that it would be a good time to stop. Same thing nearing fifty. I was high one way or another every day. It became my normal state, most people, unless they knew me well or saw me using, had no idea. Suffering from a bi-polar disorder, being high helped level me off on an up, and raise me when low. It worked, for a long time. Somewhere into middle age it became more of a problem than an aid. If I stopped drinking, I smoked more, if I stopped smoking, I drank more. If I got a prescription for pain medication, I took the pills until they were gone, paying no attention the directions. When my father died, he'd been prescribed opioids for years, for a disability he faked to get early retirement out of his state job. He began taking the pills, and besides his gambling and womanizing, he picked up a third habit. On my way to the hospital where his corpse lay, I stopped at my parent's house and cleaned out his medicine cabinet of bottles of Percocet which I consumed until gone. I didn't even like opioids, never did. But anything was better than facing life with a clear head and raw feelings. When I became a parent, I kept it under control best I could, cut down on my drinking and smoked medicinally. But I never shook it, despite the guilt and self-hatred that came with the package. This was certainly not the kind of parent I intended to be. One semester at school I taught a graduate memoir class. Three of the students were addicts, and their memoir projects were about getting clean, and their own battles with addiction. It struck me deeply. I admired them so and envied their young successes at changing their lives. During that time, I hit a major depression, riddled with huge anxiety. I couldn't get out of the spin. Unable to sleep for more than two or three hours a night, sometimes none, I was as close to a major breakdown as I'd ever been. One morning I sat on the kitchen floor—no one home, I began crying uncontrollably. I wanted to die. I thought about killing myself—no matter how bad things had been in my life—I'd never thought about taking my own life. My summer from hell. On August 27th, my birthday, I went out for dinner with my family. I drank three Manhattans and a brandy for dessert. They were my last drinks ever. I don't know why it happened then. It wasn't a plan. I woke up the next morning and decided that I would not drink for a while. But I was not finished yet. I kept smoking, more and more—five, six, seven times a day. But it did not help. I couldn't sleep. I couldn't escape my emotional state. My brain spiraled out of control, by December I was broken. I sought help, found an amazing doctor and she made the difference for me. Perhaps it was time, fate, who knows. But after a session of an abridged summary of my emotional, psychological, and addicted life, she gave me a stern warning that I was lucky to have made it this far. She could help me she promised. But only if I was willing to help myself and do some very difficult work. That Christmas day I smoked my last bowl of pot. It was months before I felt ok. I had physical and psychological withdrawal. I couldn't eat right. I had cramps, shits, nausea, anxiety attacks, couldn't sleep. But finally, the ocean liner that had been slowly turning, faced the opposite direction. The doctor prescribed medications which I took correctly. For so many years my medication use was hit or miss. I would take the prescribed medications, but usually drank and smoked pot along with them. If I felt better, I would often stop taking the meds. It was an endless, ugly cycle that took its toll on my physically and emotionally. But once I stopped using, and following the medication schedule, I began sleeping better, got back to my regular habits of reading, eating well, started yoga practice again, began writing and playing my guitar again. Life on the other side. And I could've gone to Kansas all along.

~

I knocked on the door of a little white cottage across from the harbor in East Gloucester. A small man with thick glasses and long, white wiry hair answered. I introduced myself and he shook my hand firmly. Vincent Ferrini was the first poet I ever looked up after finishing college. I came to him through poet Charles Olson whose attacks on Ferrini in the *Maximus Poems* had left me wondering, who is this Ferrini guy? I'd discovered Olson through the Beats and the seminal poetry anthology on which I had sharpened my teeth, *The New American Poetry,* edited by Donald Allen. One day browsing the used poetry section in the Harvard Book Store I came across a copy of *No Smoke* written in the 1930s, Ferrini's tribute to the people and factories of Lynn, Massachusetts. That afternoon I read it cover to cover. Along with *No Smoke* I'd found several other of Ferrini's books written at various intervals over the decades. I worked my way through them. I'd never read anything quite like that poetry—certainly in the tradition of Williams, and I sensed Robert Creeley in some places. What drew me in mostly? The poems were non-academic—as if forged out of metal by hammer or pressed out of a factory machine—products of labor. They focused on regular people, workers, factories—a social consciousness steamed inside them—as well as a touch of the spiritual—they were preachy at times—something akin to sermons. Though not the most profound poetry I had ever read—they got under my skin, these old and worn paperbacks. I kept returning to them when it finally struck me that maybe this son of Italian immigrants who'd left Lynn and lived in Gloucester for decades might still be alive. If so, he certainly would be old. I called the operator and asked if she had a listing for a Vincent Ferrini in Gloucester. Yes, she said, 126 East Main Street. I called and he invited me up. Late afternoon sun shone through the western-facing kitchen window. Ferrini drank a whiskey and offered me one which I accepted. I don't remember him as a drinker—never saw him drunk but for some reason he had one going that day. On the kitchen table sat a copy of the *Language Anthology*. At the time the book was all the rage, loved and hated depending on which side of the poetry world you stood on. I made some comment about being surprised he'd be interested. *I know what they're doing but they don't know what I'm doing* he declared at a near shout. *They're trying to suck the life out of poetry, that's what they're doing.* Full bookshelves hugged every wall. All subjects—from history to poetry, philosophy, sciences. On the few wall spaces not covered with books hung paintings and drawings. I focused on a small, wooden mask. It was pure white. *See that face?* he asked, waiting for an answer. I nodded my head yes. *Pound looks down at me from there! Pound!* We spoke some small talk for a few minutes then I asked him if he was writing. He removed his glasses, looked at me impatiently, raised the volume of his voice again and said, *am I writing? I am it! Do you understand? I am it! Life is the poem!* I seemed to have touched a nerve. He told me he got the poems that I sent. I'd mailed a sheaf prior to my visit. I asked him what he thought. He removed his glasses once more, *do you really want to know what I think—I think you need to take a good shit, that's what I think.* I asked what he meant, and he told me I was constipated. That I didn't know myself. In order to write poetry, I had to know myself, who I was, how I walked, how I breathed. *And that's all I am going to say. I don't want to be anyone's teacher. You need to find your own way.* Over the next several years, I kept in touch with him. Occasional visits. Correspondence. Our relationship remained tumultuous to say the least. He might not have wanted to be a teacher, but he sure tried. I never met anyone who seemed so desperate to tell people how to live, what they were doing wrong and how everything he did was right. I don't think he ever recovered from the Olson attack. He was defensive, aggressive, a sexist of the highest order, and a narcissist the likes I had never previously known. Yet I learned from Vincent Ferrini. A non-academic, in fact, he hated the academy though I got the sense he wanted very much to be acknowledged by them—he worked for decades at the GE Plant in Lynn. During that time he was a communist—he later became an anarchist, the first I had ever known, and a picture framer—he had a little shop beside his cottage—he'd roam the beaches and pick up driftwood to make his frames—worked as a laborer his entire life and wrote dozens of books of poetry. We remained tenuous friends until he died some time in his 90s. I'll never forget the drive back home that first day I visited him, assured that a life in poetry with a background like mine could be possible—and Vincent Ferrini was living proof.

DANTE ALIGHIERI SOCIETY 41 Hampshire St., Cambridge. 617-876-5160. **10/22:** 7:30 p.m., poets Vincent Terrini, Raffael De Gruttola, Joseph Torra and Michael Franco. Free.

~

In 9th grade I joined my first real band. Jerry Stepford was a classmate and we shared musical interests. He was the first kid at school to have his hair long and wear hippie clothes. Discovering that we both played guitar, we decided to start a band. He invited me to his house to play. The first thing that impressed me was his record collection. He had two older brothers, one had come of age in the '50s, the other in the '60s. Both of them were serious album collectors. They had records and albums going back to '50s rock and roll up through the latest music of the late '60s and early '70s. There were thousands of them. Over time I spent endless hours sitting in Jerry's living room and getting educated in rock and roll history. His younger brother was a rock photographer for the *Boston Herald.* He saw all the important bands of the time and shared his photographs with us. He'd been attending the concerts at The Tea Party for years, and more recently the Boston Garden, as the big venue shows were moving into arenas by then. That first afternoon I plugged into Jerry's amp with my old Danelectro electric Jerry was not impressed. I plucked around, played some melodies I was familiar with—but mostly fumbled. *Do you know any bar chords?* Embarrassed, I did not. Jerry tore it up on his turn. I'd never seen a kid do what he did. His playing hand flew up and down the neck. He referred to this music as "Acid Rock" though by his own admission he had never taken acid. As he played, he tilted his head back, his eyeballs rolled up into their sockets, and he seemed lost, as if in trance. I was out of my league and sorry I'd agreed to this get-together. He could play leads and intersperse them with what I learned were bar chords. Afterwards we sat in his living room. He kept playing records, louder than I'd ever heard as they had what would have been a state of art stereo for the time. We had to shout over the music to hear each other talk. I felt dejected. I thought there was no way he'd want to be in a band with me. I dared not bring up the subject again. At some point out of nowhere he said loudly: *I can teach you bar chords. They're easy. You can play rhythm and we can each sing.* Within weeks I learned all the basic bar chords and Jerry would shout out the changes to me and play wild leads to things he made up in his head. Eventually we recruited a drummer. Frank

Sarcia was a year behind us in school. To this day Frank remains my oldest and best friend. We go back fifty years. Thus, my very first band, Iced Cantaloupe was born. We performed covers of contemporary tunes—by bands like Cream, Led Zeppelin, Creedence Clearwater Revival, and even some originals that Jerry and Frank had written. Jerry learned everything and taught me the guitar parts. Eventually, we had a bass player. It was agreed that I had the best voice for singing lead, and I played rhythm and sang, or sometimes put the guitar down and sang. We played mostly local dances. It seems like it went on forever—but it couldn't have been more a year, two at the most.

~

We hid under the dining room table, fingers in our ears to cover the noise. When my parents fought, my father's anger and rage exploded through his shouting. My sisters and I huddled, tried to silence it. Sometimes they fought over money, my father's gambling, my father's womanizing. Other times we couldn't be sure what they were fighting about. Family. Friends. Old battles coming around new. My father held us emotionally hostage. No telling when he'd blow up. If they had friends over for a card game, a disagreement could turn him into a madman. I think their friends only stayed in touch because they liked my mother and felt bad for her. He never hit my sisters or my mother like he did me. Once he pushed my mother, she called the police. An officer came and had a talk with them. Before he left, he pulled my father aside. I know not what he said to him, but I never saw my father so scared. For a month or so he was on his best behavior. Until the next fight. Later I wondered why my mother phoned the police when my father pushed her but never phoned them when my father beat me with a strap. Maybe she couldn't forget the beatings her father gave her mother. Often, they fought in the car, on the way home from a family event. Something happened during the visit, and it waited until the car ride home. Nights when he worked, or went out, were the best. My mother cooked, we spent the evening in the living room watching television, eating dinner off TV trays. We had nothing to fear. I felt safe. When he was not around, life seemed pleasant and carefree. When my mother caught him having an affair with a girl in my fifth-grade class's mother, she put him out. Those weeks were the most memorable times of my childhood. Like a dream come true. If he came to the house, my mother sat in his car in the driveway to talk. He cried and begged that she let him back. We pleaded with her. *Stay strong Ma. Don't let him come back. You don't deserve him. He'll never change, never.* Eventually she caved in—petrified of a future without a husband, and her Catholicism would not allow divorce. A priest came to the house, counseled them. For a few weeks, things seemed better. But in a short time that anger returned. I inherited that rage. Spent my entire childhood and young adulthood telling myself I would never be like him. Now when that rage surges up and consumes me, and I yell and act out, as if in a mirror I see him, the electric swelling in his eyes, my own. Over thirty years dead as I write. He refuses to let go. Subconsciously I think, I became a writer because of him. He couldn't read well, nor write. Didn't know a poem from a novel. Newspapers and racing forms. Never read a serious book, had no clue about the writing world. I could be secure there. A world he could not enter, even if he tried. That place all mine—where he'll never touch me.

~

The landscape painting hung over the living room sofa. Three by four feet? A fake-gilded, ornate frame. It appeared after the remodeling my parents did in the 1970s. Paneling was all the rage for the working class. Cover the wallpaper, hang some kind of wooden paneling, install a dropped ceiling, and voila, you transformed the room. My parents had the kitchen done the same way. Installed new cabinets and linoleum floor. In the living room they bought new furniture—a recliner for my father, a love seat, chair, gold cloth sofa and a wall to wall carpet. We never had any art in the house before—the painting didn't change that. It must have been a print. It shone glossy under the glass plate. A snow-capped mountain overlooked a lake surrounded by a forest of trees—greens, golds, reds, blues, yellows, white, browns—if you squinted your eyes it all blurred together. Art never entered into the household discussions. No one ever talked about the living room painting—a decoration, nothing more. Even in the public school I don't recall a single field trip to an art museum. We did spend time each week doing art—looking back, it was more like crafts. No talk of color, composition, the meaning and purpose of art. My first public education exposure to an artform came in Middle School—music—a young, charming, attractive female teacher with a southern accent who had us read and discuss the words to the Beatles' "Eleanor Rigby." Music could be so much she told us, beyond what we think. Later that year the class made a recording—new music she explained. We listened to records that did not sound like music and we laughed. Noises. Strange electronic sounds. Disgruntled instrumentation. Shrieking voices. She set up a tape recorder, and we planned our composition—a combination of discordant sounds on the piano, bells, drumming sounds, doors slamming, footsteps on the floor, tapping on desks, vocal noises—shouts, cries, laughter. Who knows what else? *It got me thinking.* When I met Molly, who became my lifelong partner, I was in my early twenties—she knew a lot about art, music, literature and plenty of other things. In fact, the first night we hung out at her apartment, she'd just had her albums shipped to her from Minnesota. I sat on the floor, going through them one by one, marveling at the breadth of her tastes. Up to then, in my cloistered world I'd never met a girl with a good record collection. And she had shelves, with books on them. Man or woman, who collected books? I pulled out a small, thin book, *Howl*. I asked what's this? That's poetry she said, Allen Ginsberg. You like Dylan right? Well you might like that. He's a great poet and that's his famous poem. Poetry? Fucking Poetry? She took me to the Museum of Fine Arts in Boston, later the Gardner and then the Fogg Museum in Harvard Square. My whole life in Boston, first time for all three. I had no need of a tour guide, one painting after another, I couldn't believe she knew so much about all those painters. I was partial to the modern stuff but work from any period or place could satisfy. Growing up in Medford, the girls chased boys—but never me. They went after cool boys, the tough ones, wise guys and the occasional athlete. They wanted husbands, babies, apartments upstairs from their parents. Someone to take care of them. One afternoon after browsing used record and bookstores, Molly and I had lunch at one of the old joints in Harvard Square. Not sure how it came up, but I remember her saying that she didn't need a man to take care of her. She had a job, a car, an apartment. Where I came from, females were interested in getting married, having husbands that supported them while they raised families and maintained households. This was the mid-'70s—post women's movement—

things were changing—yet not so fast in certain places. I was taken aback by this independent woman who could do just fine on her own, who seemed to know so much about so many things. We became fast friends, and eventually lovers. In the beginning it confused me that a woman of Molly's caliber would be interested in a wreck on tour as myself. Evidently, she saw something. For me, everything goes back to those early days with her. She believed in me, taught me to believe in myself. Encouraged me to pursue my dreams. The more that I read, grew my interests in art, literature and getting myself off the street corner—I realized that another life could be possible. She assuaged my fears and doubts about attending college. I could do it. I was smart she insisted. Just because I did poorly in high school it didn't mean I was dumb. The idea of going to college overwhelmed me. Take one course in something you like she urged. I took a history course at night. I never looked back. In time I told her I wanted to write—she never blinked an eye. She read all my early poems and stories— bad as they were—she never ceased to encourage me. Somewhere in the universe a wand had been waved and brought us together. I was still riding a motorcycle when we met. A foul-mouthed, party-hard, full-of-myself guy—but really, oblivious. So much went on that I knew absolutely nothing about, until Molly.

~

My mother used to say that as a boy, I was either loud and silly, or quiet and despondent. There were times that I jumped out of my skin—always the jokester, trying to make people laugh and entertaining them whether they be other kids or adults. Other times a shroud hung over me. I could feel it weighing me down. Everything looked bleak. At one time during these years, when in the doldrums, I took to talking with my dog. A one-way conversation. He never spoke to me, thankfully. But I spoke to him and felt that he could understand my despair and concerns. Penny was a Beagle. She'd sit, absorb my affectionate petting and lick my face. I'd worry about school or my father or death. Share my fears with her. As I grew into my teens this stopped but not the mood swings. In those summers working long days in my father's gas station I could be playing around—driving the mechanics crazy with my antics, while on other days I'd become quiet, standing at the pumps gassing up cars, trying dreadfully to determine how many more gallons I might have to pump in my lifetime. It was not so different with my friends, these ups and downs, when I had time to be with them. They noticed it too. I'm certain that my obsession with booze and drugs had a lot to do with self-medication. Early on I realized that pot seemed to keep me balanced and my swings less severe—yet as the years passed it was not so effective. Booze simply made me feel good. Took any edge off. Once that heat in the stomach reached the brain it was all systems go. With booze, when I started, I did not want to stop. Unfortunately, the more I would drink the more uncontrollable my behavior. No matter. I never thought much about my mood swings or trouble sleeping or racing thoughts until the end of my 20s. Some days I woke up and shot out of bed ready to take on the world talking, talking, talking—waving my hands around convinced I could conquer the world. Other days I had to drag myself out of bed, everything dark—a man of very few words. As my social circle widened, I began to learn that my behavior affected those around me, how they perceived me. This was no more evident than in my relationship with Molly. She suggested that I might want to see someone, that my mood swings were taking their toll on me, her, and our relationship. At the extreme end of my swings I'd either be talking intensely, non-stop at her, hands flailing—or falling into cavernous depressions that could last for weeks—a solemn brood carved into my face—barely talking. These bouts of depression were the worst for me—the hopelessness unshakable. I recall listening to the bleak pieces of music—Beethoven's *7th*—over and over again, imagining that he knew my mind—that surely his music mimicked my own feelings and thoughts. At either of my extremes my pot intake could double, and my drinking more extreme. As a child I had trouble sleeping— night terrors were a common thing. My parents would come into my bedroom and try and calm me down. The sleeping struggles carried into adulthood, where I often could fall asleep, but within an hour or two I would awaken, plagued by racing thoughts spinning out of control. The only thing that helped would be to heavily medicate—booze, pot or both. Insomnia wrecked me. Tossing and turning, unable to stop my mind, worrying about anything and everything from things far in my past to the present and future.

~

Right from the beginning I did not differentiate between writing poetry and fiction. Kerouac wrote both. I wrote short stories at first. My very first real story was about a street person and a stockbroker who played tennis together every morning on a court along the Charles River. My very first real poem was about an old silo that I once saw while driving by a farm in New Hampshire. Dilapidated, it leaned away from a faded red collapsing barn. Early on I imagined I'd write plays too, though it never happened. I wrote poems, stories, and eventually my first novel without discriminating. Whatever needed to come, I let it. In college I read classical literature: Homer, Shakespeare, the Greeks, Dickens, the British Romantics, the Modernists, Hawthorne. At college, the poetry and fiction related to the Beats, Black Mountain, New York School or San Francisco Renaissance writers were not part of the curriculum, except for maybe Ginsberg. Any recent or, contemporary poetry that mattered came from the vein of the New Critics. I remember talking with the poetry professor and creative writing teacher—he asked me who I was reading and at the time I'd just discovered Charles Olson. He squirmed in his chair, got a look like he'd just been struck with a pain in his side, and told me he could not stand Charles Olson. Early on I realized that there were different opinions—and the teachers in the academy largely were either unaware or didn't care for writing outside the mainstream—especially when it came to contemporary work. The same teacher that trashed Olson once gave a class on the Language Poets—the class consisted of him parodying Language Poetry, writing things on the board—dictionary meanings, found snippets, words broken down into letters, and kept repeating *this is the kind of thing that they consider poetry.* He had the entire class laughing, including me—though like the time I first witnessed the Beatles on Ed Sullivan and saw how much it upset my father—I thought, maybe there is something in those Language Poets for me. I delved into the Language Poets, skeptical, and confused. Yet I could relate to their ideas that what we'd been accepting as poetry for too long was tired and worn out. I became a Language Poet—for a few months until realizing it was not for me—yet they brought me to a new understanding of what poetry could be—and more importantly, didn't have to be. It was the same with novels. In the academy any contemporary author that seemed to push the envelope was under close scrutiny, and often dismissed. I wondered how the universities could celebrate James Joyce now, when in his day they would have probably rejected him outright. Boston is a university town, and the universities have always dominated the literary scene. It is cloistered, close minded—conservative, and most interesting young writers who pass through with visions of new possibilities in writing, tend to move on. It's changed some. Over the years, students of the experimental writers have grown up with advanced degrees and have found teaching positions all over the country. Boston is no exception—but they are still the minority. I wrote many of my novels with the same nerve and reckless abandon as I approached the act of poetry writing. I've had novelists say to me that I write novels the way I do because I am a poet. Maybe. *Tony Luongo* is 218 pages of compulsive, unpunctuated prose. One long run. Some reviewers loved it. Others said that I needed to learn how to write. That's the way it is and has always been. No two ways of seeing the same thing. Art is not like sports. It's not about who wins the race, hits the most balls or makes the most touchdowns. It's about taste. As Lenny Bruce once said, sometimes it's hard to differentiate between a piece of art with a little shit in the middle, or a piece of shit with a little art in the middle. When I came of age as a writer—you had to make a choice. At least it seemed that way. Are you an "experimental" writer or not? Now, I encounter young writers who simultaneously have the most conformist to the most far out approaches in their writing. Maybe that old writing war has shifted. Today things seem to be more about identity politics, not post-modern vs. new criticism.

Dreams with teeth

a novel by
JOSEPH TORRA

A t boot camp, awaiting a posting in Korea in the mid-Sixties, Tony Luongo gets very bad diarrhoea. He lies on the ground feeling that "every last bit of my insides was oozing out of me". He runs to a stream and washes himself, filled with shame.

This visceral opening sets the tone for Joseph Torra's breakneck yet moving novel, the second of the *My Ground* trilogy about the sprawling lives and loves of an Italian-American family. Torra's focus is the underbelly of the American dream — all relayed in Tony's tough, unpunctuated street argot.

After a fifteen-month posting in Korea, Tony returns home to small-

town Massachusetts and gets a job in the local department store. As expected, he marries a local girl, Audry, and has a young son. One night something takes him over to a bar in the wrong part of town, The Other Side.

There he falls in love with the terribly vulnerable Craig. Though a creature of impulse, Tony is torn between lust and a sense of duty to the young man. The affair is tempestuous; Tony finds Craig beautiful, though he is always saving him from his self-destructive binges.

One night, Craig and Tony, who is driving but drunk on bourbon, have a car crash. Tony carries the injured Craig across town, makes sure he is OK and leaves him. They never see each other again.

The Eighties come and go; Tony prays that Craig didn't die of Aids, but sometimes when he is talking to a customer or driving the car imagines: "his light skin or his blond hair or his blue eyes or the earrings he wore when he was dressed up".

This is a blunt, slightly told tale of one man's life, but no less moving for it. It also provides plenty of incentive to find where Luongo will take the final part of this muscular trilogy.

Tim Teeman

TONY LUONGO
By Joseph Torra
Gollancz, £6.99 (Fiction)
ISBN 0 575 06848 5
£5.99 (free p&p) 0870 1660 8080

~

We all feared confession. It is where you cleaned the slate. Catholics are obsessed with sinning— there were venial sins and mortal sins. Lying to your parents—a venial sin. Murdering them—a mortal sin. In order to receive the body of Christ, or communion as they called it, we had to be cleansed of our sins. To my childhood friends and I it seemed anything fun could be considered a sin. Each Saturday afternoon we marched up to Saint Francis Church and waited our turn to enter the closet-sized dark space where we knelt, waiting for the little window to slide open behind the screen that shaded the features of the priest on the other side. I could tell from the outline of the head, and the voice, which priest would hear me and announce my penance. I assumed that the priest, with any forward thinking at all could identify me. *Bless me father, for I have sinned* I would begin. Like my friends, I never told him everything. Besides, who could tally up a week's worth and recollect it all right then and there? I kept it to the basics, standard sins like lying to my parents, swearing, taking the Lord's name in vain. It seemed to satisfy my confessors. Numbers would be involved. If I said I lied to my parents, he would ask how many times. Three sounded good and worked well enough. Without confession if you died and had unconfessed sins, it might mess things up in terms of your ticket into heaven. Unconfessed mortal sins would surely prevent any such entrance and one could spend eternity in hell—and we all knew what went on there. Even at a young age I did not understand baptism. A beautiful, newborn baby had to be baptized in order to be absolved of its sins. The nuns told us if a baby died before baptism, God would not allow that baby into heaven. Looking back, it seems like pretty sick stuff to tell young children. But at the time, everybody did it, believed in it, and at a young age I thought there might be something to it. Why would people spend so much of their time doing all those things if it were not true? And the nuns and the priests and the churches and communion and baptism and confirmation and the Stations of the Cross and confession and going to Mass? When we finished confession, we were given penance by the priest which meant going to the altar, kneeling down, and saying the "Act of Contrition" and maybe five "Hail Marys" and six "Lords' Prayers." What a great relief to rise from the kneeling position and walk out of that bleak church into the light of day. Father Foley ended everything for me. Later after talking with friends I realized I was not alone. By then we'd all discovered the mystery of sex. Our voices changed. Our balls dropped. We grew hair were there hadn't been any. And Father Foley started asking questions. He wanted to know about my thoughts. Did I think about certain things? Did I ever think about girls? Did I ever touch girls? Did I ever touch myself? What did I think about when I touched myself? Did I ever think about boys? Did I ever touch boys? That kind of thing. None of the other priests asked those kinds of questions except Father Foley. And there was something about how he asked those questions. An excitement, an urgency in his voice—elevated—especially when he asked about boys. Come talk to him he told me. We should talk more. It's important to God. I knew better. Though young and naïve—I felt certain that something was not right about him asking those questions, and how he went about asking. When it happened again, I stopped going to confession. I pretended to. I told my parents I did. I even took communion on Sundays without confession. If I died that would get me an eternity in hell. I wasn't worried. I simply had stopped believing. Not long after, I stopped going to Mass altogether except for a funeral or a wedding. The longer I remained away from the Catholic Church and its rituals, the more ridiculous they all seemed. By my mid-teens I had become a full-blown atheist.

~

I must have been six or seven. My family attend-ed one of those old-fashioned Italian parties—it might have been an anniversary, maybe a Chris-tening, when a family member or members would rent a hall or a room at a restaurant, serve food, and have entertainment. For some reason I remember a lot of blue—blue walls and multi-colored stage lights. The room not very bright, numerous tables strewn about around which families and friends sat, talked, and ate. At vari-ous intervals a band performed. My first intro-duction to live music. The band played Italian wedding band standards, "Al Di La," "Mambo Italiano," "That's Amore," with some popular music from the '40s and '50s—songs my mother sang for us. The singer had curly red hair down past her shoulders, bright red lipstick, a magnifi-cent blue dress with a wide skirt cut off at the knees, nylons with seams up the back and black high heels. When she sang it seemed that the power of the sun shone through her. That voice penetrated the room and reached into every corner, straight into my very being. Entranced, I could not keep my eyes away. Whenever the band played, I stood directly in front of her and watched. Certainly, the closest thing I'd come to sexual awareness. Like so many things that happen when we are young, I did not understand it. But the world suddenly looked different. The music, performing it, turned on her body electric. Several times she noticed how I was fixated on her, she approached, and pressing her index finger lightly into my chest sang to me. For days after I could not stop thinking about her. In my free time, at school, when I lay in bed at night. Slowly, over time, I could no longer remember what she looked like. I could only see that hair, red lipstick, blue dress, nylons with seams, black high heels, her penetrating voice and the joy exuded as she sang. My first love.

~

Sometimes it's easy to think that teaching is writing. But teaching is a job. Not writing. Not even close. Teaching is an art, of sorts. As much as I love the fact that I earn a living poring over what I am passionate about to a classroom full of students, talking about books and stories and poetry all day, if anything, it siphons off the fuel I need for writing. I had more energy and time for writing when I waited tables and tended bar. Of course, I was a younger man then. My relationship with academia is conflicted. At one time I thought the academy to be a pillar of humanity— home to truth, and dignity, a haven from the vile business of the world. Boy was I wrong. It is the place where the seedy business of the world is upheld, taught, propelled. I never set out to teach. It crossed my mind, and at one point in my life after I graduated with an MA, I sought out a PhD program. Thankfully I never made the cut. In my usual chip-on-the-shoulder manner, I told myself, fuck them and that, instead of putting all those years in jumping hoops for the degree, dissertation and then a job, I would put the time and energy into writing. And I did. That has made all the difference. But I don't want to completely dismiss the academy. There I learned to put my ideas and thoughts into order. How to pursue my passions, organize my studies and inquiries, how to broaden my vision and make some sense of literature—philosophy, art, music, history and even science. I was so in the rough, it helped boil down the wild stew, secure and steady my intellectual legs, push me in new ways creatively. Coming from my background it would have taken me so much longer to do it on my own. I had some great teachers in all subjects. They made a difference. I discovered the value of the art of teaching. There were bad teachers too, caught up in their own egos and power trips. But I also learned from them. That said, upon graduating, I realized that as an artist, there were many things I learned in the academy that I would have to unlearn and forget.

Joseph Torra's Prose and the Italian Value of Work

DENNIS BARONE
University of Saint Joseph

In her essay "Work" Maria Laurino writes that "the educated Italian-American workforce prides itself on its success in escaping the earlier fate of a lifetime in construction, and many have transcended their working-class roots by entering law and business [...]. But at what cost have we forsaken the pleasure, intimacy, and skill of using hands and heart, of expressing a part of the self in one's work?" (184-185). Boston based Italian-American writer Joseph Torra has consistently, intelligently, and eloquently written about those Italian-Americans who have not escaped (or abandoned) their working-class lives, who may still use their "hands and heart" but live on the margins of an Eataly corporate world. His protagonists are not stock exchange presidents or urban restaurateurs, but rather the restaurant

~

I began working as a waiter to put myself through college. Up to that time, I'd been bouncing around different jobs from retail, loading docks, short order cook and garage work. It took me a while to talk my way into a restaurant willing to train me. The first job was at a steak house chain. I found it very difficult in the beginning. Waiters must keep so much going on in their minds at once. I got confused, made order errors and had a hard time carrying food out on my arm as we did not use trays. It reached a point where the manager took me in his office to give me a talking to—perhaps this kind of work did not suit me. I begged for one more chance. It ended up being all that I needed. At some point several months into it I found myself moving gracefully around the dining room floor, table to table with a new-found finesse. I could carry a tray of drinks in the palm of my hand, stack dinner plates up my arm in the order that I would carefully place them down upon arriving at the table. By the end of the year I counted myself as one of the top waiters on the floor. For the next twenty or more years, I made my way from the suburbs to downtown Boston, waiting tables and bartending in some of the better restaurants around. I earned more money than I ever imagined and had the freedom over my life and schedule to finish school, and then write. I never regretted having to don that apron for the night when the next day I could be free to read, write, listen to music, go to a museum, or whatever. If I wanted some extra time off, I could usually find a coworker who wanted to pick up an extra shift. I could work four shifts a week, days free, and three full days for myself never having to worry about how I would pay the rent or keep my car on the road. I worked with writers, musicians, actors, playwrights, dancers—you name it—the perfect work environment for me. Moreover, during the '70s and '80s especially—drugs and alcohol were omnipresent in the restaurant business. Most owners and managers didn't mind if you came in high or had a drink going in the nearby coffee cup in the waiter station. As long as you did your job, no one would bother you. It is probably one of the most enabling jobs an addict could have. Everyone, from owners on down, had a taste for one thing or another. Some folks resented being a server. I learned to let the job serve my needs. As I got up over middle age, I began to slow down. I felt those shifts wearing on me physically. Customers got to me more than ever. Chefs, managers and coworkers too. Several times I had given notice and left for good only to find myself back in it. Approaching fifty I left again, not sure where to and how I'd survive. Within several weeks of my last shift, I got a phone call from a friend who was teaching at UMass Boston. They needed someone to teach a creative writing course for the next semester, would I be interested? I took the position, having never taught in a university before. And I haven't left. There were times when I found myself tempted to go back to restaurant work. So, I wrote a memoir about my experiences. *Call Me Waiter* became my way of assuring that I would never go back there again. It was all in the book—there was nothing left to write.

Joseph Torra's *Call Me Waiter*

POETRY FOUNDATION   by Daisy Fried

At 133 pages, *Call Me Waiter* is small for a novel, but no chapbook in scope. It's an account of 20 years spent working as a bartender and waiter. Torra, who's also a poet, writes wonderfully about work. Ron Silliman called one of his previous novels, *Gas Station*, "an extraordinary document…[Torra] has a real eye, not simply a literary one." There are two kinds of writers, those who want to imitate literature, and those who want to imitate life, and the second kind are better, and Torra's in the second category.

Torra's anecdotal narrative, which tracks him from job to job, is fast, clear-eyed, full of insider information entertainingly delivered. He's not particularly gentle with his characters, but he approaches them with a matter-of-factness which, however badly they behave, allows them their humanity:

Never the same after he owned the restaurant, Chub's drinking increased and he

~

Tall, heavy set, white-haired Dr. John Pierce came recommended to me by a therapist I had been seeing for anger management. I was the kid with the chip on his shoulder and later, the man with a lot of rage and anger built up inside. Not long into the process my therapist gently suggested that medications could help. I resisted, fearing that some kind of stability would prevent me from getting at the stuff I needed for writing. Moreover, it might interfere with my own process of self-medication. Like most substance abusers, I lied to my caregivers. Yeah, I always said, I did some drugs when I was young—and sometimes I drank—but not to any excess. I knew that seeing someone for medication might mean cease and desist on the drinking and drugging. So, I avoided such treatment until one day, Molly told me that not pursuing medication might end up being a condition of our marriage. Dr. Pierce was one of the smartest people I have ever known. He seemed to know about everything. He lived in a large, old house in Cambridge—a grand home, yet run down, in need of a paintjob and new windows, he told me the roof leaked rainwater into the attic. The yard was unkempt. Grass grew high and unwieldy, hedges overgrown, years of leaves layered the ground, weeds and wild bushes ran rampant. His messy office took up two adjacent rooms on the first floor with overflowing bookcases and books stacked up from tables and floors seemingly to the ceiling. His desk was excessively cluttered, and his waste basket spilled over with fast food wrappers, soda containers, paper bags and rolled up, crumpled papers. He clearly suffered from some kind of attention deficit problem, could never find anything, nor remember information unless he wrote it down. He told me long elaborate stories about his past, his childhood or college days, sitting back in his office chair, hands clasped behind his head, looking off to the distance over my shoulder. On my first visit he had me describe my symptoms. Our meeting went on for two hours. Dr. Pierce never demonstrated that he had any sense of time. That first day he asked me a series of questions regarding my life, my habits, my moods and so forth. I was honest as I'd ever been with a caretaker. At one point, he put his paper and pen down and said that he wasn't shooting for 100%, but clearly, I had some kind of mood swing disorder. There were various kinds, he explained, and they affected people differently. Mine seemed to fall into the bipolar category, somewhere between moderate and extreme. I remember at one point a glow appeared in his eyes and he smiled—it's okay, he said. Many great poets were bipolar—but he could help me. There were better medications now. It's all chemical he informed me and all we have to do is find the right chemicals for your brain chemistry. I've learned medication treatment is trial and error. I can't name all the various medications I have tried. Furthermore, in time, they must be adjusted and changed. It is an ongoing, perplexing way of life. Dr. Pierce was right, finding the right balance of meds did bring relief, and continues to do so. But nothing is perfect. Even with meds there are times when the brain waves slip through the cracks and I can fall into a depression or hypomania. One mistake that bipolar patients make—is using medications in combination with alcohol and other drugs. This compounds things—and the mix of various substances in the system can wreak havoc. The second and equally hazardous slipup is to stop taking the meds altogether. For me, this usually happened when I started to feel really good—well enough to convince myself that I didn't need the medications any longer. That I had somehow grown out of my illness. This led to a period of feeling ok and actually believing my self-diagnoses. But slowly and surely, I'd eventually begin a tailspin and spiral out of control until my drinking and drug use would steadily increase, my moods would bounce around, and my sleep become practically non-existent. Eventually I'd return to the meds and stabilize. It seems I never learned from past experiences, whenever I somehow felt normal, I could convince myself that I no longer need meds. Now that I am older, I've been able to control the habit—and it has been years since I've gone down that road. Being clean and sober has kept me on the most even path in my adult life. The dread and shame of living under the veil of my illness, of having no control over it, of knowing that for the rest of my life I will have to give myself over to caregivers and prescriptions and chemical imbalances—it's a curse, like any disease that humans must suffer. There are times when I don't see how I can do it one more day.

~

I fell in love with painting when I fell in love with Molly. Much of our time together was spent visiting museums and galleries. She was a fountain of information and I could listen to her endlessly. Molly painted and when we moved in together one of my favorite pastimes was sitting on the floor of her studio and watching her paint. I became obsessed with the relationship between forms and color, the process of working the two. In some odd way I think I was jealous. I felt that painting might be more rewarding than writing. I never had any real instincts for visual art. No talent for realistic representation. When we did some drawing or painting in school, my pumpkins or birds or trees looked dilapidated and misshapen. I had always been fond of doodling. It was a great way to pass the time when I was bored. Sitting at my desk, I drew abstract line drawings and images in my notebooks, or scraps of paper, or on my desk which I erased with spit. I'd eye them closely, not fully comprehending what it all meant but aware that these seemingly unconscious gestures evoked energy, movement and life. Later I befriended artists and when I could I visited them in their studios. My friend poet Bill Corbett was an art critic, and through him I had the chance to visit many local and New York artists. I loved seeing all their various projects in process, drawings, sketches, finished and unfinished paintings. It was so physical—you reach out and touch things and smell the paint. There seemed to be something holy about all the brushes sitting in cans or jars, endless tubes of paint scattered around in innumerable stages of use. The time-layered colors that marked various surfaces. The artists in their paint-stained clothes. Studios seemed like a shop to me—more like a place of labor compared with a desk and a computer. Closer to the garages and shops I remembered as a boy.

~

I have a lot of great stories about academia. Anyone who has worked there any length of time must. I've met numerous colleagues, teachers and administrators, most of whom are good people. While writers have always been associated with universities to some degree, by the 1980s it seemed that if you wanted to be a writer, you had to get an MFA, and if you wanted to teach, you had to have the degree and some kind of book publication(s), and it certainly helped if you knew someone. During my adulthood MFA programs have sprouted up all over the country—there are literally hundreds of them now, turning out thousands of fiction writers, poets and life-writers a year. Multiply that by one decade. The reality is that there are only a handful of good creative writing jobs available each year. For the writer who does not mind being a journey person, there are visiting writer positions. Still, even at a couple of hundred at best a year, compared with the tens of thousands of writers with MFAs growing in numbers the prospects are bleak. I don't think you can teach creative writing. I've learned that you can share your experiences, enthusiasm, passion for the written word—and offer students encouragement, permission if you will. I usually tell them if you want to write, then write, and read at least as much as you write. If you are looking for fame and fortune, you're doing it for the wrong reasons. As education has gone the way of the corporate mentality—a money making proposition that is, things have gotten uglier. Amongst the teachers, I've seen the backstabbing, pampered, self-centered aspect of humanity. It takes someone a long time to make their way to a tenured track professor—years of study, dissertation, pre-tenured track teaching and many fiery hoops to jump. Something to admire, for sure. But I've seen some of those people act so privileged and entitled. Earning good salaries, time off, complaining about and manipulating their schedules, courses they teach or don't teach, department politics, bad mouthing students. In the world of Creative Writing it seems that more often than not universities celebrate the safe and mediocre. There are very few institutions where cutting edge writers or those that take risks get the positions. Mainstream and conformist is the road best traveled. While English Departments are full of professors that celebrate deceased writers and periods of literary history—most of those same professors don't know what to do with real, contemporary writers. It's like they don't mind having the long dead, stuffed specimen they can look at behind glass, but what the fuck do you do with a real animal running down the halls? So, having the tamest of animals makes it a little easier, less of a challenge to figure out and control.

~

Instinct told me, and experience later confirmed, that writing, especially poetry, was about friendship. In my college years I began coordinating a reading series at a café in Boston. The café had a Middle Eastern theme and the owner a Middle Eastern man. He also wrote poetry and often recited poetry in Arabic. The series was a combination of open mic and featured readers. A dozen or so people regularly attended, and others came and went. Like all upstart venues, the writing was all over the place—beginners, hobbyists, and the occasional real thing—yet we all shared a passion for writing and on Saturday afternoons sat around eating food, drinking strong Arabic coffee, and sharing our work. It did not last very long, maybe a year or so, but it was a crucial time for me—desperately trying to connect with other writers. As the series wound to a close, I decided to put together a little magazine featuring many of the poets who had participated. An inexpensive Xerox project, what became *A Café Anthology* was my first shot at publishing and editing.

With that production I learned the process of making an underground zine from scratch— taking all the manuscripts, typing them up one by one, proofreading, doing a paste up, taking that to a Xerox place to be printed and collated, then stapling (later hand sewing) a cover. The reading series evolved into a publication. The importance of community was real, living and breathing. I caught the editing bug and ran with it for decades from *lift* magazine, the poetry of Boston Poet Stephen Jonas, Pressed Wafer Press and *Let the Bucket Down*.

LiftMagazine #15 & 16 (1994) William Corbett Issue. Edited by Joseph Torra. $10.00 (10 Rear Oxford Street, Somerville, MA 02143).

What may have begun as a modest midway evaluation of and tribute to Bill Corbett—poet, man of letters, and friend—has turned out to be a 150-page embarrassment of riches. It includes "Conversations" (in the form of an interview between the editor and his subject), nine new poems by Corbett and some three dozen other contributors (Robert Creeley and Philip Guston among them), represented here with poems, drawings, photographs, and other articles. *Lift* elevates Corbett to the well-deserved prominence already attained by his three new books in the past three years: *Don't Think: Look* (poetry, Zoland), discussed here by Forrest Gander; *Literary New England: A History and Guide* (Faber & Faber), and *Philip Guston's Late Work: A Memoir* (Zoland). Missing from *Lift's* treasury is Corbett the editor (*Fire Exit*) and a bibliography in progress, which, however, might have added another 150 pages to this already bursting Christmas package that arrived in January.

Cambridge. 648-2226. Jan. 15, 2 p.m., "Celebrating lift Magazine" with editor and publisher Joseph Torra and contributing editors Michael Franco and T.J. Anderson reading from their own work and work from the magazine. $4 donation.

~

I met Gerrit Lansing at a poetry reading in the late '80s. He'd already established himself as a national legend by then. Magician, alchemist, poet, scholar, gnostic, rare book collector and dealer, friend of the likes of Charles Olson, Robert Duncan, John Hammond (Gloucester castle owner and inventor of the radar system), New York School poets, painters, only to name a fraction of his connections. We ran across each other at occasional readings, though at the time I was intimidated by him thinking that someone of his ilk would take no interest in me. But gradually we began to speak to each other, and one day after a poetry reading Molly and I invited some folks to our house, and he came along. We ended up smoking pot together. I loved the idea of smoking weed with someone old enough to be my father. So erudite and sophisticated, I was taken aback at how friendly and down to earth he came off—he seemed to be so interested in me, my background, my interests, my writing. So, we became acquaintances. I remember driving to Gloucester one day with several other local poets and visiting him in his bookstore, Abraxas, on Main Street. Our friendship became sealed later when Gerrit bought his fabulous house, what became a school for so many of us, at 207 Western Avenue, overlooking Gloucester Harbor and Stage Fort Park. Gerrit needed help packing books into boxes from his older, small place where he lived with his lifelong partner Derek. There were several of us out in the garage where Gerrit had thousands of books shelved. At one point, Gerrit packed a box of books, then went to fold the top parts of the cardboard box over and tuck them in. He stood next to me, and fumbled about with the top of the box, as if confused. Then he asked me, *Joe, how do you fold the top of a box to keep it closed*? My first thoughts were how can a person so smart and enlightened not know how to fold the top of a cardboard box? Then I thought maybe he knows how to fold it and is trying to bond with me and make me feel relaxed with him, as if he could learn from me. I never did figure it out. But I have never forgotten that day, and in that moment when I bent down and folded the four flaps of that box and he watched me, then tried one for himself, we were friends for life. As time passed, we saw more and more of each other. Gerrit became an intimate friend. For years I visited him in Gloucester, often sleeping over—in the guest room during cold weather and in the small cabin that sat behind his house in the good. He'd always have the bedside table set up with books for me—maybe some obscure Taoist text and a rare collection of Chinese poetry. Early morning found him outdoors in his yard calling to the birds.

There is no calculating the hours of conversation and exchanges we shared over the decades. A self-proclaimed Taoist and lover of Chinese literature and philosophy—we were bound at the hip. But there was so much more—his knowledge was encyclopedic. With friends, or new acquaintances he always seemed to be more interested in them than talking about himself. He loved children and became a lifelong friend of my daughter Julia. He'd get right down on the floor with them. Immerse himself in their world. We loved wild mushroom foraging, and spent incalculable hours together in the forests around Cape Ann. He had long stopped drinking, having nearly drunk himself to death as a younger man, but he always had booze in the house and offered it to me. He loved pot and we would smoke late into the night and converse. For a while he used marijuana tincture and when I'd arrive, he'd be waiting in his kitchen with a dropper full. *Put your tongue out* he'd say childishly. Before his health got in the way, he made frequent trips to the city to visit friends and the Harvard Library. I'd meet him in Harvard Square for lunch or pick him up there and take him to my place or a local Somerville eatery. Early on he became a reader of my work, I always sent the new manuscript of a novel, or poem drafts to him and he read with a close eye. The greatest writing compliment I ever received came from him. He once told me that he believed I'd reached a masters level with my writing. Gerrit was not one to hand out compliments lightly. He lived a fascinating life, and while he shared many things about it with me, he disliked being interviewed and always dismissed any suggestion that he write his memoirs someday. But these are just small pieces of something so large. Gerrit was the most important and influential friend I have ever had. To me, he is a Taoist Immortal. He remains with me—he's just not *here* anymore.

Gerrit and Julia

~

It took a long time to learn how to teach. I'm only an adjunct. At UMass Boston they like to call it Non-Tenure-Track. But a horse is a horse. In the early years I went on my nerve. Like I did in the beginning with writing. Trust your instincts. I taught from my own library. Photocopied hundreds of pages of poetry, short stories, essays. My lessons were freewheeling. The first course I taught for several years, Introduction to Creative Writing, covered poetry and fiction. We read poets and fiction writers in every class. There were no formal writing assignments. Students could work in any genre they chose, as long as they wrote both during the semester. Write and turn something in every week was the plan. Write what you want. Eventually, as I read student evaluations and talked with students, I realized for newer writers, they needed more structure. So, I began to give them writing assignments too. I brought them writers that I love, old and new. Same to this day. Teach what you love. I learned as I went, and it went on for several years—sometimes striking gold, other times falling face down in the mud. After five or six years, I finally felt I had some sense of my job. Get them to read and understand the fundamentals of technique. Moreover, trust your instincts, write what you need to write, and more importantly, how you need to write it. Sure, poets should learn the basics of form—meter, rhyme. Yet, just meeting the rules does not make a poem. There are myriad bad formal poems. As many as in free verse, probably more since old forms have been around so much longer. Besides, most of the forms taught were English, the great colonizers—why impose a colonizer's form on my poetry? Same with fiction, understand the basics of story and novel writing. But don't let that confine your prose. What is the idiom you speak I ask my students? What is the language that you grew up hearing? How can that influence your poetry or prose? How does your mind work? How do you walk? How do you breathe? What, as Charles Olson asked, is your *stance towards reality?* I have a penchant for visiting the local Italian cafes. As the old timers die off, so go the cafes. I'm not talking Starbucks or the local hipster joints. The Italian cafes are the places where no one is online, or on their cell phone, or writing their latest novel or poem. There is one in particular I still frequent when I need to get in touch with my roots—on Mystic Ave. at the Malden/Medford line. The clientele is made up of old Italian immigrants—men who speak what I call *goombah*. It's a hybrid of broken English and Southern Italian peasant dialect. They talk loudly, at a near shout—a music score grounded in emotions, rising and falling, rolling rhythms, staccato, starts and stops as they conduct themselves with waving hands and arms. They're usually not talking about anything important—though American and Italian politics occasionally pop up—but more likely they're engaged in topics like what kind of macaroni their wives will cook that night. This is my language. The music I first became aware of sitting in that highchair a long time ago in Medford. I relax, take it all in, it's occasionally so loud when the place is full it becomes a deafening pitch. This is not iambic pentameter. Free verse is another kind of verse—with its own responsibilities and risks. This is not Henry James. This is *Tony Luongo*, ranting away, waving his hands for 218 pages of unpunctuated prose.

~

Boston's North End is seminal to my early, formative years. Now a gentrified tourist attraction, when I was a child it was a real neighborhood. During the 1960s there were still Italians emigrating to the country, and in Boston, they first settled in the North End. My own family had lived there when I was a baby, before doing the immigrant hop out to East Cambridge and eventually Medford. My grandparents remained there, along with some aunts, uncles and cousins. Whenever a new extended family member moved here from the old country, the North End was the first stop. Once my family had left we still spent much of our time there. On Sunday mornings I drove in with my father to visit his parents, other relatives and friends. I accompanied my mother on her shopping days. During the summer I would stay for extended periods of time with my grandparents. I hadn't yet learned about the potential troubles my grandmother could bring. She was an oversize woman with crystal blue eyes. She spoke no English, and I very little Italian. We communicated through physical and vocal gestures. Same with my grandfather. He seemed tall to me then, smoked a pipe and treated me fondly as we shared the same first names. Fascinated by his pipe, he would let me hold it unlit, and put it in my mouth.

At my grandparents' place in the North End

I slept between them in their double bed located in a small bedroom. I don't know how we fit but we did. In the morning my grandmother would send me down to Bova's Bakery for a warm loaf of fresh Italian bread. I'd return and we'd slice the bread and eat it with jelly, she'd put milk in a cup and add a little espresso which they brewed in an old-fashioned pot. I'd add sugar and enjoy my own special coffee milk. My grandfather would take me to the Parado, a park on Hanover Street behind the Old North Church where the statue of Paul Revere stands. I'd hang out with my grandfather and all his old Italian cronies. Some days my grandmother would take me and my cousin Vinnie, who lived on Salem Street, to the North End Pool. She'd pack a lunch for us of thick-cut crusty slices of bread stuffed with meatballs, and fruit. I'd carry her folding chair and she'd sit with all the Italian mothers and grandmothers while Vinnie and I would swim and play with kids he knew, Vinnie was always quick to point out pretty girls in bikinis. Sometimes we would sneak on the subway, Vinnie taught me how to run under the turnstile when no one was looking, and we'd ride a couple of stops to Downtown Crossing and roam around in and out of Filene's, Jordan Marsh or a pawn shop. Vinnie took me to the Combat Zone where we'd look in porn shop windows or photos of women on posters hanging outside of strip bars. Eventually someone would run us off, often a po-liceman. My grandparent's apartment had no shower or bath. Like many of the old timers, they went to the public shower. I remember my grandmother taking me in the women's shower and having me shower with all the other naked women, including herself. My father's godfather Rocco owned a pastry shop on Hanover Street. Rocco's Pastry was the most popular around. There were no tourists, but Italians from the suburbs bought their pastries and special event cakes at Rocco's. As did all the locals. I remember young man who worked for Rocco named Mike. He had been my mother and father's best man. He would later open his own pastry shop and now he is world famous. On days leading up to holidays when the shop was extremely busy, my father would take me to Rocco's where they put me to work washing and scrubbing pans. I loved watching the bakers make all sorts of pastries: neapolitans, cream puffs, bombolone, sfogliatella, biscotti, cannoli, rum cakes, fruit tarts. No sooner would I clear one stack of pans in the oversize aluminum sink it would fill up again. There were always men coming to visit Rocco and they would go to his office and close the door only to emerge an hour later. I think Rocco wore many hats. When I think of the North End now, I see woman hanging out of windows shouting out to each other and others sitting on folding chairs on the sidewalk. I remember my cousin and I roaming the streets and alleyways day and night, the parks, Copps Hill Cemetery where Vinnie stashed his girlie magazines behind an old gravestone, making scooters out of wooden vegetable crates we found at Haymarket, nailing the crates to a two-by-four and attaching roller skate wheels to the bottom then flying down steep Snow Hill Street. During the feasts my cousin and I carried the blanket ahead of the saint's statue at the parade, people tossed coins in, or little girls were held up to pin bills on the saint's clothing. I remember the smells emanating from apartments, gravies simmering, meat and fish frying, the aroma of garlic, the strong smell of coffee from the cafes, the garbage bouquet of alleys or the bread baking from bakeries. Italian was the language spoken. All the adults spoke it, shopkeepers too. I was an outsider. The few words I could muster were hardly enough to make me a real Italian. I rarely go there now. It's crowded with tourists, very few Italians actually live there. The old buildings have been rehabbed. Apartments are now spacious and expensive—some turned into condos. There were hardly any restaurants when I was a kid. Mostly neighborhood variety stores, religious shops, butchers, bakers, storefront cafes that fronted gambling joints. Now there's a restaurant every which way you look, and the little shops are gone.

~

When Dr. Pierce died, I received a letter from his wife. He went suddenly, unexpected—she was sorry to have to break the news and would be certain to make sure all of my records from the doctor would be made available. Pierce had left a major impression on me—I'd been his patient for years—I got the sense that he liked me, to talk with me—there'd be times when I remained with him well over my allotted time conversing about various subjects from Asian philosophy to litera- ture which he especially loved. He was clearly better read than I. He forgave me when I didn't take my meds properly or took myself off them altogether—always patient to get me back to a regular schedule and make certain that I became stabilized. Pierce believed our mental issues were mostly chemical. Yeah, things that happened to us when we were young had some bearing—but mostly it was all hard wired from the start. Our brain made us do things no matter how much we tried to force it otherwise. *You can put a monk in a monastery, but you won't stop him from mas-turbating* he was fond of saying. When Pierce died, I went through a long period—years, of bouncing around with psychiatrists. The biggest problem is not only finding one that takes insur-ance—but also taking on new patients. There's nothing more humiliating than the search for a mental health care giver. It's a social stigma—even in the health care industry, it's not like ad-mitting you have a physical illness. And you are constantly reminded of it. Another problem is finding a doctor who really cares and can help you effectively. There were numerous quacks I encountered—some wouldn't listen to me—others watched their watches and whipped off prescriptions haphazardly. I remember one that gave me some free samples to try that I realized later were expired. This made it easy to self-medicate—to try different medications—stop tak-ing them—use them in combination with alcohol and pot—the entire circus. Most of them didn't notice or didn't care. As mood swings fluctuated my substance abuse remained constant. It was years before I found another doctor who cared enough about her patients, determined to help me bring my illness under control and stop drinking and drugging. I was ready to be com-pletely honest with her. The right place right time kind of thing. She would do all the work necessary she promised, but I had to take that first step I'd been avoiding most of my young and adult life—stop self-medicating. When I finally found myself in her office, I was at a lifetime low—something inside me was ready to make a huge change. And I did.

~

One autumn brought one of the most productive mushroom foraging seasons ever. My interest in foraging began when I was a child, and my father would take me rabbit hunting with his Italian American friends. We'd drive out to the far suburbs, at the time large woodlots and farms—yet to be sold off and divided up for middle-class housing developments. Most of the men kept beagles, as did my father. We'd release the dogs in the woods and fields, and they would bark their hound-sounds and echo through the woodlands while we waited at strategic locations for a shot at a hurrying bunny. Other times we drove up into northern New Hampshire and the deep woods and mountains where we hunted the hearty jack rabbits. One thing was a constant: mushrooms. No matter the harvest of game, the real prize seemed to be wild mushrooms. I can still see the excitement in one of the hunter's eyes, emerging from the woods. *You otta see the mushrooms I got!* Back at camp in the north, the cleaning of game and mushrooms, everyone fueled with red wine, capped an end to a magical day. Later, I gave up hunting and sold my guns. But something about the change of seasons, the crisp air, the green hardwood trees turning yellow, orange and red—it got under my skin. I began foraging for mushrooms again. Each season is different, there are mediocre years, dry years, and banner years. You take what comes.

Mushrooms are mysterious. They seem to be not of our planet. But the chase is all, walking the

woods amongst birds and wildlife, the ever-
greens and hardwoods, weeds, swamps, bogs,
ponds, forest air—it's why I go. And the taste,
when the foraging is productive and I bring the
fruits of my harvest home, clean them, dry them
or freeze them to cook later in omelets or sandwiches or stews or just plain sautéed with a little
butter, salt and pepper and good bread. Never
gets old. As November approached that year,
putting an end to one of the best and memorable
mushroom seasons ever, I found myself in a
good place emotionally I'd picked way more
mushrooms than I needed and ended up giving
some away to friends that I knew would appreci-
ate them. Little did I know that within a month
I'd be in a freefall. It crept up slowly on me.
Around Thanksgiving I found myself growing
irritable. That familiar gloom descending over
me like a shroud. Except for when my children
were young, as an adult, I'd never been one to be
excited over the holidays. That December the
very thought of Christmas brought a sinking feeling in my stomach. I'd been having trouble sleeping and it only got worse as the month wore on.
By Christmas and New Year's Day I had nothing
left. I had all I could do to get myself up in the
morning and face the day. It had been a long
time since my mood took such a serious swing. I
was in a deep depression, with full blown anxiety. I'd alienated friends, and my behavior at

home had put me at serious odds with my family. Sure, I could always apologize, tell them I am sorry for my erratic behavior—but year in and year out, as hard as it is on me, I know how hard it must be on them. My caretaker helped. I'd been slow to report my changes until it was too late. Medications were adjusted, and in a matter of a week my disposition shifted. I began to sleep better, the old glass looked half full rather than half empty. I felt ok in my skin, I started writing again, practicing yoga, reading, and by the time the Spring semester started at the end of January, I was stable. But two months of my life were lost in this helpless tumble that is part of being bipolar. From a magnificent fall of woods walks, mushrooms and nature to tossing and turning in the middle of the night in a full-blown panic unable to fall asleep. There's nothing in life I despise worse than knowing that even with medication on board, when the lightning strikes, I will burn. I have no control over it. Yes, it will pass, but in the meantime, the only thing I can do is live with it. The ups are fewer now, especially as I get older. When young, and premedication, I had the energy and physical stamina and could focus enough so that while I was capable from bouncing from one idea to another—I could also turn that hypomania into novels. I could write the draft of a novel in a matter of months—doing the bulk of my work during the sleepless nights, often fueled with coffee and pot. But in the end, I grew out of that, and those old tricks didn't work any longer. The older I have grown, most of my swings take me down. The ups are not nearly as intense, and all too brief to put to good use. Not using substances has made a difference exponentially. Drinking and using during depression, over time, just made those bouts worse. When on an up, pot seemed to have little effect, while booze became a matter of more, more, more. Now I take what comes. I let the medications do their work without augmenting things. If I feel good, I enjoy it. When I feel bad, I know it will pass. Altering those states in any manner will only set me up for an emotional hammering I can no longer swing.

~

Gerrit Lansing introduced me to Stephen Jonas. Molly and I were throwing a party after a reading. It was the early stages of my friendship with Gerrit. He asked me if I'd ever heard of the poet and I told him no. I wouldn't have Gerrit explained, most of his work was out of print and not many people knew about him. He was self-educated, gay, mixed race and at the time of his death he hadn't been a household name in poetry. Jonas had lived at various locations in Boston, a friend of Gerrit's, known only within a local circle and a handful of New American Poets. Gerrit filled me in about Jonas. He'd published in some significant little magazines. Friend of Boston poets John Wieners and Joe Dunn. Part of a legendary group of mid-'50s Boston poets that included Wieners, Dunn, Jack Spicer, Robin Blaser and Ed Marshall. He'd published two books of poetry later in his life, but they were out of print and hard to find. Gerrit said *I think you'd like his work*. It happens that just a few days later I was visiting Bill Corbett. I asked him if he knew anything about the Boston poet Stephen Jonas. Without a word Bill turned towards a nearby bookcase, looked for a moment or two, reached up, pulled out a book and placed it in my hands. *Exercises for Ear*, by Stephen Jonas. On the subway ride home, I opened the book, and during the remainder of the ride, and the duration of the day, I was consumed. The poems were pithy, gritty, sassy. They seemed to have so much of the qualities I loved in William Carolos Williams' poems—with a jazz beat. They were fragments, starts and stops, often trailing off unfinished. Like a jazz saxophonist riffing off short bursts and moving on to something else—improvisatory and spontaneous. Some were highbrow and I could sense a classic sensibility, others were of the street and the lowbrow. They were about Boston, sex, drugs, people on the fringe. These poems were Beat—of the New American Poetry. I wanted more. When Stephen Jonas died of a drug overdose in 1970, his apartment was full of his notebooks, papers, letters and manuscripts. Before everything got tossed in the apartment clean-up, Gerrit Lansing and another friend collected all the papers. Eventually they were made the literary executors. Everything was stored in cardboard boxes that Gerrit kept in his basement. By the time I first got my hands and eyes on everything the boxes were dilapidating and many of the papers thin and faded. At the time I was editing *lift* magazine, and when I learned that all the work was out of print, I asked Gerrit if I could make a selection of poems and put them in an issue of my magazine. He answered with an emphatic *yes*. It seems there was so much poetry there I hardly knew where to begin. Later, when *lift* evolved from a xerox zine to a desktop, bound, published journal, I decided to do a double issue dedicated exclusively to Jonas's writing. I'd been digging deeper into the Jonas papers, familiarizing myself with them. There were long poems, short ones, the *Exercises for Ear* and a long epic poem titled *Orgasms*. The *lift* double issue brought Jonas back into the eye of the poetry world. I remember when I finished with its production, my old friend Bob D'Attillio who helped with the design (the new technology was beyond my skills) told me to put a box of them away because someday they would be worth money. Twenty-five years after the fact, used copies occasionally surface on the Internet for as much as $150. The *lift* Jonas double issue led to a contract with Talisman House, publishers who wanted me to edit a selection of Jonas's poems and write an introduction. The work brought me even closer to Jonas. Gerrit Lansing allowed me to bring all the papers and notebooks home and for the next two years I pored over the work in my studio. At one point the complete edition of Jonas's *Orgasms* (all the various poem versions) was spread out on the floor. Jonas rewrote many of his poems, so in many cases there are numerous versions of short and long poems. My task in the beginning was to determine which version Jonas would have wanted in print. In some instances, he dated things so that I went with the most recent. Other times I went with the versions of poems he saw into print in his books or in the variety of literary journals that had published his work. One of my biggest problems editing Jonas has always been spelling. Jonas often spelled certain words by ear. At the same time, I believe he typed at lightning speed and that might lead to typos. Again, I went with the spelling of words of poems that he saw into print. Sometimes I went on a gut feeling. I also had to face the fact that during certain periods of times Jonas had anti-Semitic views and they found their way into some of the writing. He called Chinese "Chinks" and Italians "Dagos." Most of the anti-Semitics came from his reading of Pound, whose economic theories Jonas embraced. Moreover, in addition to serving time in federal prison, Jonas had been hospitalized with mental health issues. I'm not sure if there was ever an official diagnosis. It seems to me he could have been manic depressive as he could get lost in long bouts of deep depression or hit ecstatic bouts of mania where he would be up for days and hear voices. This is not an excuse, but it is not uncommon for people who suffer from paranoia to seek out particular groups as enemies. I think that could be, at least partially, the source of his racism. It's interesting that I found the majority of his racist rants in his longer works, where the writing could become incoherent, products of Jonas's sleepless nights and manic driven writing. The Talisman House book brought Jonas's poetry into an ever-widening circle. For years I gave talks and readings, sat on panels as the interest in Jonas grew. Last year the great City Lights Press brought out *Arcana, A Stephen Jonas Reader* which I co-edited over the course of several years. It was the apex of Jonas's long slow comeback into the poetry world and nearly 30 years, half my life, of editing the work. It began with a tip-off from a couple of friends, developed into what became an apprenticeship into the world of poetry. The work continues. Just this year I gave at talk on Jonas at the University of Pennsylvania.

~

We never learned about class in school. For the most part the textbooks ignored it. The long and ongoing struggle with the Native Americans is whitewashed. I learned that slavery did exist, but Abraham Lincoln freed the slaves and racism a thing of the past. It had been fixed. There was a time when children worked in factories and mines, long hours in unsafe conditions. But that was changed. At one time women could not vote but now they can. The books taught that those things occurred in the past, yes, yes, we had that then, but we corrected it. And that was that. We never studied the trajectory of slavery, labor, the ongoing condition of Native Americans, complete equality for women, the implications of class—it seemed as if no ripple effect existed—a line was not drawn between then and now. We teach writing that way too. So often I hear among the writing worthies who flourish in academia, that modernism, experimental writing, free verse, writing outside the accepted forms, has been done. As if they are saying, like ending racism, yeah, we did that. The implication is that a return to the old forms is a rational and logical move for writers and students of writing. I see it the other way—we've already had centuries and centuries of the old forms—the new forms are still babies. Don't they deserve to grow? But if we teach writing the way we teach history, be it labor, gender, race, class, etcetera—we are essentially teaching that there is a vacuum that is not important, and when we ignore the history in the vacuum, we can essentially maintain the status quo. I encourage my creative writing students to find their own voices. I believe that is the most important thing they can do. Sure, have an understanding of form and established narrative techniques—use them if you wish—in your own way. But to follow them as a poetics or practice in and of itself, is to shut the blind eye on racism since slavery, the problems in labor since the labor movement, the struggle for women's equality since the suffrage movement, the implications of class on our social culture. In a sense, we make state sponsored art, the same way we educate with state sponsored curriculums.

~

I discovered yoga at middle age. My late nephew, then a practicing Buddhist, turned me on. Having failed at meditation, I was seeking some kind of practice that would tone my mind, body and breath. Tai Chi had appealed to me as it is generally practiced in China by Taoists—but something about it just didn't fit. While yoga originates in India, early on I felt that it made sense to me. Like tai chi the emphasis was on the mind, body and breath. On another level it seemed to be about liberating the mind and body and unifying it with a kind of universal absolute. As it happens Gerrit Lansing, a longtime practitioner of yoga had studied the philosophy of yoga and he became a great resource. Molly had long since passed a book along to me called *Yoga Self-Taught*, by Andre Van Lysebeth, one of the early Western experts on Hatha Yoga. To this day the book sits on my night table and I open it regularly. There is no end to the correcting and fine tuning of postures and practice. Over a five, or six-year period through trial and error I learned the routine that I use to this day. Year in and year out, I have improved. It's a natural progression. But the basic Sun Salutation and nine postures (asanas) have not changed. For years I continued to drink and use substances, yoga remained an off and on practice. Even with the toxin residue in my body I noticed benefits. It was a good cure for a hangover. I often smoked pot then did a yoga session. Whenever I did, I noticed a difference. My mind seemed more focused and my body more limber. I often wondered—if I could feel this good after a session now, imagine how good it must feel to do it with a clean mind and body. My practice came and went—stepping it up and at times losing touch—but it never went away. Getting clean and sober is an endless complicated process. In the early stages I had all I could do to make it through each day. The urge to read, write, play music or do yoga didn't enter into it. In time, the body and mind begin to change. Activities that it seemed I'd lost all interest in suddenly wanted back in. Not all at once. One day I found that I had my guitar in hand. Another time I'm drafting out a poem. Then one morning I'm doing Sun Salutations. Since then my yoga practice has become a constant. My practice has become so much part of my life, more than any time since I began. My brain is clear, my body is toned, and muscles stretched, my sleep is improved. At this time in my life I average six mornings a week. When I miss a day, I can tell. My energy level is off, my brain is not as focused, my breathing is not as regular. It's not that I jump out of bed ready to go. There are mornings when I feel sluggish and need to give myself a mental push. But once I begin my mind and body thank me, and early into the process everything kicks and an I know why I do this. I will never be a yogi, that's for sure. My age limits what I can do, and I trust those limits. Yoga centers me. If feeds my creativity. Like my vision of the Tao, it liberates my mind and body, and unifies it with the cosmos.

~

As a young writer I lived it 24/7. There was always a stack of five or six books I read my way through, and an on-deck pile that grew and grew. I listened to music, went to view art, hung out when I could with artists in their studios, went to see dance performances, plays, concerts, poetry and fiction readings. I associated with other young writers and most of our time and conversations were spent in passionate discussions about writing, art, and music. We argued, agreed, talked enthusiastically about the future and what we could do as writers to be a viable part of it. I worked as a waiter, had yards of time free and pursued my dream of becoming a writer as if my life depended on it. A sense of urgency drove it all—as if it were the only thing that mattered. Every new writer that I discovered, contemporary or older, led to four or five more writers in my on-deck pile. There seemed to be no end. My life's path spread out ahead of me like a yellow brick road. I had no time to stop but to grab everything within reach before it got away. This went on for years. I truly believed that writing could not only change my world, but the whole world. I pursued it like some noble, holy endeavor—an art, like all art, that would remain pure and uncorrupted. It was a divine time in my life. I never knew such purpose and passion. I'd found my way into a sacred circle. These were the formative years in my writing life. I wrote poems, stories, novels—I edited and published magazines. Several nights a week found me at a reading, or a gathering of writers where we practiced the life of writers. About ten years into it, after many missed steps, false starts, and fall backs, I saw something in my poetry that I didn't recognize. The poems began to appear less imitations of what I thought I should be writing. It scared me. I'd written a serial poem of about twenty-five pieces I called *the domino sessions*—and all I could do was put it away. They couldn't be any good if they didn't look like the poems that I thought I should be writing. One day after about six months I took them out of my desk drawer and gave a look. It didn't take long to realize that I'd finally written poems only I could have penned. Sure, they had their antecedents, but these were mine and mine alone. Thus, the beginning of the end to my decade long apprenticeship. I wrote on my nerve from then on. No care of what I thought I should be writing. Not long after, I wrote the first draft of *Gas Station* in a matter of weeks.

The Written Word

Josephine Foo and Joseph Torra—3/27 at 8: Josephine Foo's first book, entitled *Endou: poems, prose, and a little beagle story,* is a collection that includes a range of work from lyric poetry to quixotic cartoons. Joseph Torra is the author of two collections of poems: *domino sessions* and, more recently, *Keep Watching the Sky.* The Poetry Project/St. Mark's Church, 131 E. 10th St. (674-0910); free.

The Best American Short Stories 1995—3/27 at 6:30: *The Drowning* by Edward J. Delaney, as read by Malachy McCourt, and *Pagan Night* by Kate Braverman, as read by Maria Tucci. Jane Smiley is the host for the evening. Symphony Space, 2537 Broadway (at 95th St.) (864-5400); $16.

Susan Sontag—3/28 at 7: Introduced by Elizabeth Hardwick. Tishman Auditorium, 140 Washington Square South. Free.

Macdara Woods—3/28 at 6:30: Author of *Notes from the Countries of Blood-Red Flowers* reads from *Selected Poems.* Glucksman Ireland House, New York University, 1 Washington Mews (998-3950); admission $5; students admitted free of charge.

Louis Gluck and Robert Pinsky—4/1 at 8: Reading at the 92nd St. Y, at Lexington Ave. (996-1100); $12.

~

Completing *Gas Station* was a milestone. Years of reading, writing, living my life as I supposed a writer should live life, I finally saw the results of all my efforts. Trying to live the writer's life, no matter how dedicated, did not make me a writer. But having a finished manuscript in my hand, a book that despite the influences of all the writers, that only I could have written—it mattered most. I could do it. I'd done it. The proof was in the pages. Exhilaration. A satisfaction and feeling I had never known. I sent the book off to Roland Pease at Zoland Books, publisher of my first book of poems. Zoland Books was a small, independent but respected press founded by Roland. He was a kind, generous man, and I am forever grateful to him for believing in me and giving me my start. He wrote back immediately saying he loved the book and wanted to publish it, and if I was good with that, he'd have it out within a year. All the years building up to that seemed to finally pay off. But once I did it, once I'd actually written a novel, there was also a kind of let down. It seems we are only writers when we are writing. Now that I knew I could do it, I needed to write another one. The mad obsession with all the gatherings, writer talk and designating my artistic boundaries about what mattered and what didn't, seemed much less important. I *was* a writer. I had no more need for the training I'd undergone for the past ten years. Be it a poem, or a novel—the puzzle had been completed. Writers write. Community, socializing, letter writing, praising all the great writers whose work inspired me, reading—you name it, you were not a writer unless you wrote. And writing is work. So many people have told me that they have a great idea for a story, or that some day when they have time, they will write a book. In my mind, ideas entertain, offer hope that lives in our minds like fuzzy dreams. But ideas do not write books. Once you are an adult, unless you have some kind of trust fund, you will have responsibilities and bills and time-eaters that devour free time like ants on a piece of bread. No one will ever give you the time you need to write. You must make the time. And it's never the same writer to writer. Middle of the night. Four in the morning. An hour at the end of the day. Sure, retreats and colonies can offer you a week at some cozy place near the ocean, or in a lovely hilly forest with someone knocking on your cabin door at noon offering a box lunch. But you still have to go back to real life. And it's mostly impossible to write a book in week. Or, you can hope for a grant that might give you enough money to survive for a few months or even a year. But in the end, it's back to regular life if you plan on being in writing for the long haul. You've got to find a way to pay the bills and find time for writing. For me it was the restaurant business, and eventually, teaching. The problem with teaching is you can succumb to the false notion that teaching creative writing or literature is the same as writing. But when you get home at night and you've been reading student poems or stories or essays on literature—see how easy it is to turn the computer on and pick up where you left off. Not very.

Reading at COLLECTED WORKS
THURSDAY   7:30
JOSEPH TORRA
reads from his new novel
GAS STATION
(Zoland Books)
Reception in The Cafe Beyond follows the reading
COLLECTED WORKS   29 High St.
Brattleboro   (802) 258-4900

~

After *Gas Station* was published I continued writing. I wrote the *Bystander's Scrapbook*, *Tony Luongo* and *My Ground* over the next few years. My publisher at Zoland Books committed to bringing out *Tony Luongo* as the follow up to *Gas Station*. During the editing of the book, we hit a wall over an editorial disagreement. Not worth getting into specifics here. Suffice to say he wanted me to make an editorial change and I didn't agree. We went back and forth over the next few weeks until finally he gave me an ultimatum. I made the changes, or he would not publish the book. I walked. Some friends said I was crazy. That the change was not very significant, and I should not give up my book deal over it, especially since Zoland was interested in future novels of mine. To me, being an artist is about freedom. It's the only place in my life where I am totally free to do whatever I wish. I would not compromise that freedom. So, my contract was voided, and I moved on. I have never regretted that decision. That said, for the next several years I could not find a publisher for any of my books. At one point I signed with an agent who promised me she would get me out of the apron when she learned I worked as a waiter. She delivered on none of her promises as publisher after publisher rejected me. I kept writing, waiting tables and tending bar while unpublished manuscripts piled up. Going from all the fanfare and critical "acclaim" over my first novel, to a novelist without a publisher was a letdown for sure. But I'd made a commitment to writing years before and wouldn't stop. Even if I never published again. Fate intervened. One day in London, England, Ian Preece—a young fiction editor at the legendary Victor Gollancz Books, walked into a foreign book store with his wife. As they looked over the offerings, Ian's wife noticed a copy of *Gas Station* displayed on a table. She picked it up, walked over to Ian, put it in his hands and said this looks like something you might be interested in. Not long after I received a letter from Ian introducing himself. He asked if anyone had rights to publish my book in Europe, and if not, would I consider Victor Gollancz. He loved the book and had already talked it up with his superiors. Ian turned out to be my angel. During the contract signing time, we had a phone conversation and he asked did I have any other books. I told him I had three unpublished novels on my desk. Send them he said. I don't know how he did it, but a few weeks later he contacted me and told me Victor Gollancz would like to publish all four of my novels. Over the next several years, my books were published in England, distributed in Europe, reviewed favorably and I went on as an unknown writer waiting tables in America. I'd all but given up hope until down the road the small presses gave me a life, and PFP Publishing brought out the *My Ground Trilogy* (*Gas Station, Tony Luongo, My Ground*) under one cover in the U.S. But I can't help but wonder where I'd be if a young London editor never walked into that foreign book store.

~

To this day I have no recollection of painting for the first time. What drove me to start picking up paints is a mystery. Sometime around middle age I found myself with some paints and brushes and setting up some blank canvases in my studio. I had no idea what I was doing. I knew from watching Molly paint that you could mix different colors and create other colors. While capable of fine drawing skills, her paintings were abstract, and she'd put one line down and follow-up with another. It reminded me of the improvisatory elements of jazz, or the Projective Verse concepts established by poet Charles Olson. Spontaneous, organic, urgent—one gesture led to the next. When she did something she didn't like, she worked it over. Sometimes after a day or more of working on one painting—she'd cover it all over with gesso because she was not happy with the results. In the beginning I opted away from abstract. I needed something to fix my focus on. I painted large outlines of recognizable shapes and filled them in with smaller versions of those recognizable shapes. One of my very first "keepers" is sitting on the floor in front of me now. It's a solid blue background with the solid black outline of a house sitting on a descending dark slope. Inside the outline of the house are dozens of versions of various smaller houses in an assortment of different colors. Roofs, chimneys, doors, windows, walls, red-brick, domes all clustered together. I titled it *Model Homes.* I've never had any inclination to sell paintings. I occasionally give one away to a friend if they really like one. It's actually difficult to part with them. When I finish one that I like I can't imagine letting it go. I want to hang on to it, even if the only person to see it is me when I pull it out on a whim. It took a while to learn how to use brushes and paint effectively. There were lots of failures along the way. But the paintings began to evolve, they became less representative, and eventually I found myself in the land of the abstract. It's no wonder. The New York Abstract Expressionist painters had always spoken to me. They seemed like a natural progression from the Modernists. I loved the amount of emotion and energy they created. Echoes of Jack Kerouac's writing, or a John Coltrane solo. There's a great satisfaction that comes with painting. Setting up the paint, prepping the canvases. Getting into a painterly mess and then cleaning everything up when finished. I love staring at the paintings in their different stages. At any given moment it will pop into my mind and I'll sneak into my studio and have a look at what's there and think about where it might go. When I'm working on writing, at any given time I might suddenly think about a passage or a scene and turn it over in my head. Same with a painting, there are mornings when I wake from sleep and see a particular palette and forms in my head. I go through different phases, where a certain group of paintings share similarities in their concepts and forms and composition. Eventually when I've worked through that period I move on. More than writing or music, there's something extremely visceral in the process. It's deeply rooted in my Taoist practice and studies. Something about the nature of existence and its interconnectedness with the cosmos. When I paint I feel as if I am cultivating my original nature. Thus, many of my painting titles come from Taoist concepts, I use and re-reuse over time: "The Great Clod Burdens Me With Form," "Emerging and Returning," "Energy Assembles Becomes Essence," "Burgeoning Forth."

~

Slowly my activity out on the scene began to wane. By the time I became a parent, between parenting duties and holding down a job as a restaurant server, I would be too tired to write or didn't have the blocks of time. Moreover, what spare time I had I preferred to spend with my children. That would only come once. Over time, Julia grew eager to hang out with my friends and attend poetry readings or visit an artist's studio with me. I learned that writing can be done in short bursts—an hour here or there, a half an hour in the morning before sunrise while everyone in the household slept. For prose, some days I might shoot for five hundred words, or as little as one paragraph. This meant that the project grew, however slowly, and I could maintain a connection to the work. In terms of poetry, I could always take a notebook out and tinker with a line or take the poem through another revision process. When the girls grew a little older, I could withdraw for an hour or so, tell them unless the house was burning down, *don't bother me.* In time they needed me less and less in the moment, more chunks of time opened up and I took advantage when I had the energy and drive. Most of my novels were written in bursts. Never more than two or three hour runs, at times closer to one. On the occasions when I was experiencing hypomania from my bipolar disorder, I could stay up at night, an old-fashioned espresso pot on one side of me, my bong on the other. I wrote in the dark, with only the computer screen for light. I wrote madly and desperately—each project seemed to demand its own method. I went were it took me. I'd write poem drafts anywhere—on cocktail napkins while bartending, in my head while driving, in notebooks at the breakfast table, at my office desk in the university. I took them when they came. I learned early on I wasn't one to get up and simply write poetry every day. As Jack Spicer put it, I was a catcher. One thing for certain, my activity out and around the local literary scene became less important—I no longer had the time or interest. And over the years I have become disenchanted with the scene. I've learned to hate the industry that has taken over writing. Now the poetry biz disgusts me. All the contests and prizes and grants, who they go to and why. There are hundreds and hundreds of them from the little chapbooks to the big-name presses and the older established and most prestigious prizes and awards. And let's not forget all the contests with reading fees... Are there really hundreds of writers that good, each year? To what goal all these accolades? Toward the purpose of the daily business of the Creative Writing Industry. The mighty state of the Associated Writing Programs. It all seems to have lost touch with the original spiritual center of creation. There seems to be a fundamental dislocation from the natural process that brought humans to the cave walls to paint. We have become separated from that natural process. Product over process. That writing world that I imagined, fantasized about, so desperately wanted to be part of is a lie to me now. This does not mean there are not good writers writing. Or that we should not write. But the life I once lived, seven days a week, all waking hours, is a distant memory—like periods of my childhood hard to grasp at all—that bottleneck of time chokes the past the older I get. The purpose of writing blurs in my imagining.

~

Last night I attended a memorial for one of my two great writing mentors, Bill Corbett. Pancreatic cancer took him in August of 2018. Bill was the kind of person who touched a lot of people's lives, not just writers and artists. The turnout was huge at Grafton Street, an eatery and pub in Harvard Square where Bill frequented, usually with a group of enthusiasts around him. A large, boisterous, complicated man, people either loved Bill Corbett, or they didn't. If he took to you, believed in you, liked you—he would do anything for you, and you were welcomed into his always widening circle of friends. If he didn't like you for whatever reason, he might be cordial, but basically ignore you. Bill took to me immediately. I don't know why. When I first met him, I had no chops as a writer—my excitement, enthusiasm, passion for life and writing must have been evident to him. *Be true to your vulgarities* he was fond of saying. It made sense to me, helped me overcome the shame of my background in my

155

new and evolving circle of friends. And I liked to drink, one of Bill's many passions. We shared a love for music, writing and art. So, in no time this in-the-rough working-class kid from the street corners of Medford found himself sitting at the now celebrated dinner table of Bill and his wife Beverly, at 9 Columbus Square in Boston— next to painters, musicians, poets and novelists— some of international notoriety. I was not the only one of my kind, the Corbett house was a nexus for all kinds of people from all backgrounds. Somewhere in the cosmos a wand had been waved and the universe blessed me with one of my two great teachers. I don't mean university professors. Yes, they can be of some use and importance. But for them, it's a job for which they get paid. The real-life mentors are friends— there's a human connection that isn't officiated by some institutional authority. You meet for coffee, drinks, lunch, dinner, long phone conversations, correspondence, discussions about life, art anything. They support you. They give you permission to write. We read each other's work. I first met Bill at a reading in an art gallery in the South End. He read with two other poets who eventually became friends—Fanny Howe and Margo Lockwood. Being in an art gallery, Bill began his reading with Frank O'Hara's poem "Why I Am Not a Painter." I'd never heard a reader read someone else's poetry before. Early in our friendship I asked Bill about this, he explained that he felt no different from jazz musicians who might play their own tunes but also play standards. He saw those poems he read as standards. Bill also had wide tastes in writing. He might read Elizabeth Bishop poem in his set, and a Charles Olson poem. As he always insisted, poetry should be about more not less. Not long after that gallery reading, we crossed paths at a Robert Duncan Memorial. We continued to acknowledge each other at the reading series, usually with a nod hello. I gave one of my earliest readings at this same series—Bill in attendance. Afterwards he came up to me, shook my hand and said it was good to hear me, that I had some good tones, rhythms and sounds. *Tones, rhythms and sounds.* That's how he complimented my poetry. Those words were etched into me. In time I learned that music mattered so much to Bill, not just in poetry, but in life. We shared more time than I could recall talking about music, listening to music. Jazz being his first love, it could be opera or pop music too—he was a real musicologist, his collection so extensive. His tastes and knowledge were encyclopedic. If we were out and about and walked by a music store, he would run in spur of the moment, clack the CD racks and leave with a handful of new discs, often handing one off to me. Before CDs he collected records. It was the same with books, he couldn't pass by a bookstore without stopping in and dropping some cash, again, gifting me with one of his purchases. Bill had a steel trap memory, could talk endlessly about music, art, writing, baseball—he loved the Red Sox and visiting Fenway Park to watch the games. He knew more writers in his life than I can possibly imagine—from the rich and famous to a poet who lived in the street around Harvard Square. He ate, drank and talked with such passion and intensity—like no other person I have ever known. He came into my life at a perfect time, and gave me permission to write, and be true to the person that I am. *Be Joe Torra* he taught me, *write what Joe Torra can write*, don't worry about what anybody else writes and don't compare myself to any other writers. Bill and his wife Beverly were famous for their dinner parties. Beverly had a flare for cooking tasty meals for large groups of people. And I mean large groups. Despite the fact that they lived in a brownstone in Boston's pricey South End, they'd purchased the house in the late '60s when it was practically ghetto. By the late '80s when I met Bill, gentrification had set in. The Corbett house, or Chez Corbet as some of us called it, was caught in the middle. Valuable artwork hung on the walls, there were lovely sitting/living rooms on the second floor decorated tastefully. Bedrooms and Bill's office were on the third and fourth floors in various stages of needing work. Bookshelves stood on all accommodating wall spaces, Thousands and thousands of books. The first floor consisted of a Beverly's office in the front room, and a medium sized kitchen in the rear. Despite the Corbett's passion for throwing dinner parties, they had no dining room. They had dining table that sat between 8-10 comfortably and took up a good deal of the space in the kitchen. But often those dinner parties consisted of twelve, fifteen or more people. At times, there were so many you could not move, and the table so cramped we were elbow to elbow, hardly a bit of space to access your plate. Those parties grew more boisterous and heated as the wine flowed. I met so many people at that table. I'm not interested in name dropping but I met the rich, famous and not so. The Corbett's prided themselves on hosting a diverse group, but I eventually learned that the worthies got the better treatment—in terms of attention, and food. Beverly's menu had a marked difference when someone of importance sat at the table. So many well-known writers, artists, musicians, celebrities, a famous local weatherman, who remembers who else broke bread in that room. The conversations were lively, interesting and intelligent with laughs aplenty. Yet most of my best time with Bill happened one on one. Our lunches, phone conversations which were regular, often daily, and went on sometimes for an hour or more. Or my trips with Bill, rides down to New York City, or up to Gloucester to visit Gerrit Lansing or to Lowell to visit Kerouac's grave. It seemed like Bill was less pressed to be "on" during those times. Occasionally he could even be vulnerable. I think Bill had a desire to be of a higher class, though he came from solid middle or better—the son of a doctor. Beverly had come from money—my sense is that it was the tail end of what was once a good deal of wealth. Bill seemed fascinated by people with money. One day when we were hanging around NYC together, we came out of the MET and Bill insisted we walk down Madison Ave. He wanted me to see expensive shoes. We went into several shoe stores, where the cheapest pair were in the multi-hundreds and some up to thousands. In each store, Bill tried on a pair with the higher price tag. It seemed he got great pleasure out of pointing them out to the salesperson, saying he'd like to try one in his size, which he did, walking around the floor for a short time, looking at them in the mirror. He wanted very much for me to do the same. In my converse high tops and grubby jeans, I couldn't bring myself to do it—way too self-conscious and embarrassed for such a game. He and I were friends for nearly 30 years. I suppose I could write a book about our relationship. Sometimes it could be rocky—Bill wasn't always the easiest man to get along with. Like most alcoholics, he could be temperamental depending on his emotional state. Mornings were probably his worst time until he got his first glass of wine into him at lunch. I had my own problems. We both had father issues, serious ones. That might have been where we connected. Bill became a regular reader of my work—both poetry and prose. We edited *Pressed Wafer* magazine and press together. When I edited *lift* his input was invaluable—same, especially in the early days, when I began to edit the work of Stephen Jonas. His reputation as a teacher stretched far and wide. I can't count the number of young people who were affected by studying with Bill. Not just writers, but people who went on to have careers in other fields—science, business, medicine. *He was the most important teacher I ever had.* Time and time again that's what I heard. My very last conversation with Bill was by phone, it went on for a long time—he was sick with cancer by then and living in New York City. I was teaching a course that I had never taught before and had some questions for him, and he turned it on until he'd exhausted his recommendations and advice. Bill, I believe, had a hand in me getting my job at UMass Boston. He was a great source of information in terms of how to approach teaching, what worked for him and what didn't. On numerous occasions he brought me in to be a guest speaker in one of his classes. His rapport with students was phenomenal. I owe so much of my writing, editing and teaching to Bill. There were times when he hurt me. I know there were times I hurt him. Personality issues. Alcohol issues. No need to get into specifics. Despite the times we fell out, love kept us coming back. Socially, I think he seemed most comfortable when he was in command of the conversation. If he slipped out of the loop, he steered things back to him. He liked to be in control. There was no other way for him.

Bill Corbett

~

While I think it is important that every writer have a mentor—I think a friendship with someone closer to your own age is also vital. I've been lucky enough to know dozens and dozens of writers of my generation. Many have become friends. But none like T.J. Anderson III who has become like a brother to me. I met him in the mid-'80s when I attended UMass Boston as an undergraduate. I'd heard of T.J. through the student vine, but he was a year ahead of me and we never crossed paths while in school. One night I attended a party thrown by a fellow student. There were lots of folks in attendance, including a number of students associated with UMass. Somehow, I began to talk with this fellow and when we introduced ourselves it turned out to be T.J. I'd heard of him I said, and he told me the same. That meeting changed my life. T.J. and I talked all through the night. I remember we appropriated, or stole, a bottle of brandy that was in a cabinet and went outside on the back stairs of the apartment. I had pot and we smoked and drank brandy from the bottle and discussed everything under the sun: politics, music, art, writing, academia (of which we both held doubts), religion, philosophy. From then on, we became best of friends. We talked on the phone, hung out, often at my apartment as at the time he lived with his parents temporarily. We listened to music, talked, smoked pot, shared our poems and planned our futures as writers and how we might change the world. We turned each other on to writers, and explored new writers, musicians and artists. It was a furious exchange. We were near the same age, both at the beginning of our careers, and the love, support and belief we had in each other made all the difference. I would never have made it without him. Alone, I might have tried, but together there was no denying that we were going to do it, and we were going to follow our dreams and faith in the kind of art that meant something to us. While we had differences, one thing was clear—we each had a disdain for the mainstream dreck of the day—the university sponsored poetry—still under the influence of the New Criticism. We would rather die than write that. My whole life I have remained in Boston. T.J. is a traveler—he left Boston for Providence, later Michigan, lived in Cairo, and eventually settled in Virginia. Nonetheless we never lost touch. Before computers and email, which was when we were sharpening our teeth—there were letters. A great, lost art form in itself. We wrote to each other regularly—sometimes daily—hardly a day passed when there were no letters of ours in the post traveling back and forth. We eventually named our correspondence the Chorus-Pond-Dance.

with T.J.

Those letters became a bond I needed to survive. We shared drafts of our poems, reading lists, music listening, everyday news. There are hundreds and hundreds of these letters—I've never taken the time to count them, but they sit in sev-

165

eral boxes in my basement. We were young. We were crazy for life, art, music, making a better world through our writing. Very few people write letters these days. My own letter writing life dwindled down to a trickle with the dawning of the email. Now T.J. is a full professor, co-raised a beautiful family, practices meditation, is a musician, has published numerous books of poetry and criticism. Our communication has been reduced to occasional phone calls and emails. But nothing will ever separate us. My life has never been the same since that night on the back stairs of an Allston apartment. I had no idea what was in store. All of us, I believe, need someone with whom we can forge ahead from nothing into something. A hand to hold. A friend to love. A life to imagine.

~

Sometimes I sit back and look over my life. As a kid I'd been told one way or another, that because of my social status, I'd never amount to anything. Part of me believed it. I spent a lot of years during my youth and young adulthood trying to figure out what I could do. What I could do meant one thing: a job. I tried many in those days. No matter the work, not long into it, things became impossible. Whatever the job in no time the daily grind beat me down. I worked in retail, I worked on loading docks, I worked in garages, I was a short-order cook. How could I possibly do this day in and day out for the rest of my life? No matter how much I worked I never made enough to finance anything more than meeting the monthly bills. By the time I paid rent, groceries, gas, car insurance, bought some clothes and maybe went out once or twice during the week, no funds remained. Often, I'd have to borrow a ten or twenty just to get to the next paycheck. Worst, I felt empty and desperate—the days long and tortuous—the weeks endless. The weekend passed far too quickly and back to the Monday morning. It seemed to be what everybody did. Sometimes I thought I'd rather be dead. When I started reading, suddenly there was a new light on horizon, yet I could not decipher what was out there. At the same time, my everyday life grew more unsettled. At times I'd think back to when I was a kid and watched *Hard Day's Night* and remember the freedom with which those four young men lived. Writing songs, playing music, never a dull moment. Did anyone really live that way? During that period of my early 20s the only thing that relieved the boredom and desperation was when I went out to see bands. At the time a thriving local scene had emerged and everywhere bands were playing highly charged rock and roll that had become known as punk. Folk music really, simple enough for non-professionals to sit around in a living room or front porch and play. But now it was electric, loud and fast and folks were banging out three chord songs at local bars and people in the audiences danced wildly in response. The new punk heroes Ramones had a line in a song that went: *"Gabba Gabba we accept you we accept you one of us."* Anyone could join. Everyone accepted. Like me, so many of the fans, as well as the band members worked dead end jobs during the day and I'm guessing to one degree or another felt as shitty about it as I. But this new scene, this new sound, was liberating. Anyone could play it in a matter of weeks. Anyone could dance to it—even if you could only jump up and down. It put a bug in my head. I began playing my guitar again. I was renting a house with several people and we'd jam in the living room at night, playing rough covers of songs old and new—"Louie Louie," "Hang On Sloopy," "Steppin' Stone," "You Really Got Me." At the time, it never jelled into anything commanding enough so that we could play out—but inside me things were swirling. Creating music. I felt on the verge. Of what I did not know. But I could taste it, smell it, feel it when I reached out to touch.

~

The Beats brought me the poetry and philosophy of the Asians. Kerouac's *Dharma Bums* for sure, which led me to Gary Snyder, Phillip Whalen, Zen, Buddhism and eventually Taoism and the poetry of China. Kenneth Rexroth's book of translations *100 Poems from the Chinese* was an epiphany. He'd overseen the infamous Sixth Gallery Reading where the Beat writers read, and Ginsberg publicly unleashed *Howl* for the first time. I'd read his *Collected Longer Poems* and *The Collected Shorter Poems*. Eventually I discovered Ezra Pound's *Cathay*. I still have that book of Rexroth's translations, as well as his translations of women poets of China. Worn, and fragile—both as vital to me as they were over thirty years ago. There was something about the economy of language in those poems—and how much those poets were able to charge the language with thought and feeling. The deep image. The intimacy with the natural world as well as the common everyday experience—how they were seamlessly interwoven—grounded by a philosophical sensibility that I could not yet name or know, but I felt it. There was an inter-connectedness of the human, natural—and time seemed to lack a past present or future for a kind of all-time-one-time. It felt so right to me. Kerouac, Ginsberg, Snyder and Whalen led me to Buddhism. Buddhism led me to Zen. Then Tao opened up to me a new ontology—one in which I wanted to live and exist. One that really didn't have a name, nor could it be articulated. The closer I came to a definition, the farther away it slipped. I bought my first volume of a Taoist text, the now ubiquitous, oversized volume of the *Tao Te Ching* translated by Gia-fu Geng and Jane English. Now I have numerous different translations. From there I traveled to the *Chuang Tzu* where I swirled about in a world of parables and allegories many of which left me scratching my head until over time some of them became clearer and left me seeing the universe and my place in it in a new way. Eventually I discovered the *Lieh Tzu*—the trilogy was complete and for the past twenty years there has never been a time when I am not deep into one translation or another of those texts. This is no Catholicism, with right and wrong and a perfectly mapped out dogma that I have to follow in order to avoid the ferocity of hell for an entrance into an eternal afterlife with all the other good people and an all-knowing creator. Here any God that can be named is not the real God. Here eternity is all-time. In the end the beginning. In death life, in life, death. And this kind of thinking underscores the poetry. The Rexroth translations led me to the anthology *Sunflower Splendor* which introduced me to the breadth of Chinese poetry—three thousand years of it, one dynasty after another. The translators varied. I had no idea of the quality of them. I read in no particular order. I'd jump from one section to another. I had no idea about the historic chronology, and which poetic elements might be unique for that particular time. But one thing for certain—the poems had many elements in common: sun, moon, death, war, love, nature, friendship, drinking, hunger, oppression, exploitation, the changing seasons, a human being's place within the universe and more. As the years passed my fascination with the Chinese grew, the more I learned about Chinese philosophy and history, the more I understood the poetry. Little by little I began to make sense of the chronology of the poetry, going back to the *Book of Songs* and other folk poetry to the poetry of T'ao Ch'ien, considered the first lyric poet to create a poetry in his natural voice and write about his personal, immediate experience. From his poems an entire tradition of Chinese lyricism was born. Of course, Li Po and Tu Fu being the most celebrated of Chinese poets were the first that I read in any depth. My love affair continues to this day—over thirty years long—and I am yet to exhaust the myriad voices to be read. At one point, so deeply under the spell of the Chinese, I began writing my own poems in the manner of the Chinese. Other than the character for *man*, I could not read a word in Chinese. But riffing off all the various translations I had, I jumped in, making no intention of calling my poems translations. In some instances, I took titles, or lines or phrases straight from a translation I had—and used them without credit. I jumped from one period or poet to another, freely. In a few instances, I used material from more than one poet in a single poem. Some would say I should be ashamed of myself. Perhaps. As time moved on and I continued to read deeper into the Taoist texts of Lao Tzu, Chuang Tzu and Lieh Tzu, my notion of my own place and time and purpose slowly shifted. *After the Chinese* aside, my most Chinese influenced work is *Time Being*. I was raising children, deeply connected with the domestic experience. Women poets such as Bernadette Mayer and Sung Dynasty poet Mei Yao Ch'en were much on my mind—rather than get side-railed by the domestic demands—those duties simply became material for the writing. Molly worked days, I worked nights. I changed diapers, did laundry, cooked, cleaned, went grocery shopping, took the kids to school and doctor and dentist appointments. Those chores found their way into the writing quite naturally. I set out to write a one-year journal. Write anything and everything that seemed to need to be written. I would approach the project as a musical improvisation— whenever I sat down to compose, I wrote what was on my mind and occurring around me. One thing just flowed into another, coffee with a friend, a conversation, something I overheard in public or during a class, discussions with the kids, dreams, my mother fading into Alzheimer's disease, recipes and meals cooked, my Taoist readings. Anything that wanted in, got in. I did very little revision in terms of content. I saw the piece as a poem consisting of one long line. Others, including my publisher, saw it as a prose poem. It never mattered to me what anyone wanted to call it. The only part of revision that concerned me once I finished the draft had to do with syntax. In unpunctuated works, as in many of my poems and my novel *Tony Luongo*, getting the syntax right is everything. It's hard to pinpoint exactly what I mean when I say this is the most Chinese book I have written. It seems obvious to me, yet, impossible to explain fully. It has to do with time, and the Chinese philosophy of time. Or should I say no time. While the book has a chronological trajectory of one measured year, the narrative encompasses all time. The lack of punctuation renders it difficult to discern when one situation or event ends, and another begins. Written in the present tense, it's one long continuum, abiding by occurrences appearing of themselves. It's an all-encompassing present—a constant *burgeoning forth*—a continuous transformation or unfolding, past, present and future. A vast organic process. I see it and feel it in that book. I didn't intend it or set out to do that—but somewhere along the way during the writing it became obvious, to me. This morning I continued reading recent translations of *Analects* by Confucius. Of all the Chinese philosophers Confucius is the most difficult for me. Short aphorisms, one after the other. The emphasis on the social ritual—slips through my fingers like trying to hold water. But still I pursue, awaiting those rare moments when something sparkles, like a shiny flake on a beach of sand. I used to dislike Confucius—I saw him as a tool of oppression—but as time goes on I realize how much of his thinking has been selectively usurped and changed by the powers that be to be about submission to authority and oppression—much like religion in Western Civilization. In reality, it seems to me that Confucian thinking is to the social realm what Taoism is to the private, spiritual realm. This all said, the closer I find myself gravitating towards Chinese culture—the more I find myself grounded in Western culture. *A pure product of America gone crazy.* As a Chinese friend once told me—I am not Chinese—I am an American through and through. Funny how I often laugh at the New Age followers who have embraced Eastern Religions and customs and abandoned our own. I am doing the same. But the Taoist ontological stance continues to fascinate and inform my life. I am, after all, only a drop of water.

~

After graduating high school my activity playing with bands slipped away. By the mid-'70s, totally enraptured by the punk movement, and the local Boston scene, I lived with a group of people all of whom played and sang to one degree or another. We jammed a lot at the house we rented, tried to get something off the ground, but never enough to play out. From then I was a guy who kept my acoustic guitar always within an arm's reach, could play a fair number of cover tunes from early '50s rock and roll through the punk craze. I spent a lot of time alone, smoking weed, drinking, and strumming—but other than the occasional booze-fueled, weekend living room jam with friends, that was the extent of it. By then I was immersed in college, writing my earliest poems and short stories, not thinking too seriously of being involved with any kind of band. Things remained that way for a long time. Once I began writing fully in earnest, graduate school behind me, all my creative energy went into reading and writing. Poems, stories, attempting novels. I still enjoyed going out to see live shows, and music continued to be a huge part of my life. But playing in a band had become a memory, and I never imagined getting back to it. As I approached middle age, when most folks would be hanging up their instruments or band dreams for good, I got hooked. I was working at a restaurant bartending and waiting table. As it turned out, a lot of my colleagues played instruments, had been in bands, and were excited about music. We intended a one-off the first time we gathered. One of the bar tenders had played bass, and she and her husband, a musician, and his brother, also a musician, rented a house together. They had a practice space in the basement. We all met one night: our chef, an experienced drummer, a line cook—who played keyboards and sang, Melissa, the bartender on bass, and me and another waiter on guitars. We played for hours, cover tunes, old and new. Sloppy for sure, whomever could recall the chords passed them on to the others and we each sang what lyrics we could remember. Something sparked inside me that night. Pounding out those chords and singing and feeling the bass and drums filling me up from inside I felt as if I were seventeen again. We agreed to meet the following week. In no time everything jelled and before long I began writing songs, something I had never done before, and the keyboard player wrote some too. In a matter of months, we'd evolved into an originals band. We played shows at local clubs and recorded some of our originals live in our rehearsal studio. Since then I've been in numerous bands over the years. It's not that I have any designs on being a rock star. The energy and thrill of rock and roll is something primitive. A rush I can't compare with anything. Not like writing, or even painting—it throbs up from the lowest levels inside me and needs to be shouted out to the world. Or the twenty people on any given night when we play in a bar.

The First Supper with Hugh O'Connell and Levi Rubeck

I learned the art of recording in my band Box. We recorded two eleven song CDs. Each one took over a year from start to finish. I wrote all the songs. Lead guitarist Mark, who I'd had the pleasure of playing with for years, had recording and production chops and a studio in his basement. My songwriting took off. A Dylan I wasn't. But I had a flair for to-the-quick songs—a melding of pop/rock/punk tunes—formulaic for sure—two verses, a chorus, occasionally a bridge, a quick guitar solo back to a verse and chorus and out—all in about two and a half minutes. I wrote about my life.

Rather than go back and write love songs from a young man's point of view I wrote from a middle-aged guy's point of view. Putting the lyrics and music together came quite naturally. I remember practicing guitar in the living room one day, plugged into my Marshall amp, banging out some power chords. My daughter Julia was there watching me. I wondered what she thought of her old man. Thus, my early song "Daddy's Got a Marshall" was born. A song told through her eyes, watching her old man rocking out in the living room. *"Daddy's got a Marshall/He's rocking through the day/It only takes three chords/And he can chase those blues away."* I've written dozens and dozens of songs since then. To this day I remain a member of a band—turning seventeen every time I plug it in.

~

I often find myself telling younger writers that once they finish their university studies, the hardest thing to do is to keep writing. No longer do you have a story or poem due for your workshop, or teachers prodding you along, or fellow students who share the same interests and like you, want to be a writer. The world doesn't need more writers. You've got to pay your rent and support yourself which requires a fulltime job which can and will sap all your energy so that the last thing you want to do at the end of a long working day is write. Your school friends will have moved on and be stuck in the same situation as you. Many former MFA students I encounter and ask about their writing lament that it feels like something of the past. They don't have time, or energy, or a reason. One thing that can save you is community. This can come in the form of one person, or a group—a few folks that meet once a week and share work. You can start a little magazine which will keep you in contact with other writers. You can start a reading series. These things guarantee an exchange with other writers even though editing a magazine or curating a reading series are thankless tasks. You'll find there are invariably more people wanting to read in your series or publish in your magazine than want to support you. I was lucky enough to wander into the Word of Mouth Reading Series after I had graduated. I'd been working in the restaurant business. I attended local readings, but most of them were unexciting and demonstrated little enthusiasm for the kind of writing that interested me. Most of them were associated with the local universities and academic circles that were closed shops. Published poets only—award winners—professor writers. When poet Robert Duncan died in 1988, I attended a memorial reading at Word of Mouth, a fairly new reading series in Cambridge. It took place in the basement of a restaurant. The room was full of writers of different ages, all of whom shared similar tastes as mine. I met many area writers that day, many of whom became lifelong friends. The series supported the kind of poetry that had come to mean so much to me—there seemed to be a line that stretched from modernists like Williams, Pound, Stein and the Objectivists up through the New American Poets with a nod to Language poetry which was all the rage, or scorn at the time—depending on which side you were on. This poetry had traditionally been ignored in the Boston area. For the next several years Word of Mouth became my school, and the community that I had been lacking, and seeking to find. Local poets read, out-of-towners read, young and newer writers read with older established writers. What most of them had in common is that they were writers who would not find acceptance or a reading anywhere else in town. We participated in literary events such as a reading of the Olson-Creeley-Corman Correspondence; performances of Gertrude Stein's plays; a complete reading of Jack Spicer's *After Lorca* and an afternoon of the poetry of Stephen Jonas just to name a few. Every reading a local artist brought paintings or drawings down to hang for the afternoon. On some occasions the paint still wet! It was a small community, but a community for all of us. We began to socialize, going off to bars for drinks and food, hosting dinner parties and gatherings at our homes, meeting for lunches or coffee or drinks. In time I began *lift* magazine picking up on all the energy and activity of Word of Mouth. *Lift* connected me with newer emerging and established writers, around the country and even the world. This was a hugely important part of my development as a writer after finishing college. I believe this is what all newer and younger writers need, community. Community can be many things, for me, there is a good chance that I would not have made it as writer if not for Word of Mouth and *lift* magazine. As Neil Young sang, *all my changes were there.*

WORD OF MOUTH READING SERIES Tapas Restaurant, 2067 Mass. Ave., N. Cambridge. 648-2226. $4 donation. Dec. 18, 2 p.m., "A Bernadette Mayer Read-In," with Clark Coolidge, Joseph Torra, C.D. Wright, Michael Gizzi, Patricia Pruitt, Peter Gizzi, Christopher Sawyer-Laucanno, Lee Ann Brown and Elizabeth Willis. $10 donation.

WRITERS AT WATERSTONE'S BOOKS 26 Exeter St., Boston. 617-859-7300. 7 p.m. unless noted. Free. **2/18:** Andre Dubus III ("House of Sand"). **2/19:** Boston Review Fiction Contest Winners: Jacob Appel and Rhoda Stamell. **2/23:** Word of Mouth Presents Joe Torra, Ed Barrett, and Patricia Pruitt. **2/25:** Suzanne Vega ("The Passionate Eye").

~

Early in our relationship, Molly and I had decided that we would not have children. At the time, it was something we were both ok with—and we felt that if you don't want children, you probably shouldn't have them. Things went fine, as we pursued our interests and enjoyed our leisure time together. Over time, things shifted, especially for Molly. Approaching middle age, the topic returned to our conversation. I resisted at first—my writing career was finally getting underway—publishing books, editing journals and editing the poetry of Stephen Jonas. I feared that children would get in the way of all that. Besides, I never had a model for a father. I worried that I would not have the skills to be a proper father, and I would inherit all the negative energy from my own father and pass it on to my kids. Molly was adamant, she wanted children, and would have them with or without me. And so, over the course of the next several years we adopted two daughters from China. Once I accepted the idea, while my fears remained, the idea of children grew more appealing. International adoption is no small thing. It is a long, slow, frustrating process filled with endless bureaucracy in the U.S. and the country from where you are adopting. There were times when I never thought it would happen. But eventually, in 1996 Molly and I traveled to China to adopt our oldest daughter Julia. And again in 2000 to adopt our second daughter Celeste. As soon as they placed those girls into my arms, I felt they were mine. I never saw the racial difference, and I realized immediately that taking care of them seemed to be a no brainer. You loved them, nurtured them, respected them, and made time for them. I wonder why my father never had the right stuff. I'll never fully understand how being confronted by his own flesh and blood he could not love, he could not parent. I have been a flawed father and made the same mistakes my own father had made—but there is no doubt in my mind that having children was the single most important thing I have done in my life. There are so many memories— great, good, and awful. So many they just turn about my consciousness in flits and flashes. Yeah, there were the shows on Broadway and the trip to Disney—but the quiet moments, the thoughtless times are the best. Feeding them breakfast, Julia leftovers from dinner because she hated breakfast food, Cereal or an egg on toast. Preparing school lunches and dropping them off to school. I remember as a kindergartener Celeste was so small her backpack seemed bigger than she. Watching them week in and week out at Kung Fu lessons, or music classes and recitals, holding Celeste in my arms when she was sad and cried. Taking a woods-walk with Julia foraging for mushrooms—naming a trail we visited regularly "Julia's Loop." Leaving them off at college and crying the entire ride home. I'm sure all parents must have such experiences. They are innumerable. As a kid I remember a television ad that said being a parent was the toughest job you will ever have. No doubt. Everything shifted once I became a parent. It was no longer all about me. I am lucky in that Molly is a great mother. She inspired the girls by example to be independent and empowered. Fortunately, there were two of us. I know a lot of single parents and can only imagine the difficulties. It seemed Molly and I each had our own positive things we brought to the parenting process. It made a huge difference. The girls are grown up now. Fine young women both. Sometimes I wish I could sit through one more Kung Fu class, or cook one more breakfast, pack their lunch and drop them off at school. Memory is all. But to love and be loved by them is the most pure, joyful experience I have ever known. One time I talked with Julia about my addiction problems, and how I regret those years when I was using and not being responsible. She replied—*it's ok Dad, you were always there for us, even when you were high.* How does one deserve that kind of love and forgiveness?

with Celeste and Julia

~

This morning is gray, overcast, humid though not hot. Earlier I sat out on my front porch with morning tea and watched a rabbit scamper around the patio. They are everywhere in the city this year. I returned inside to read from a David Hinton's translation of the Confucian *Analects*. It is a difficult book for me. I don't find it humorous and rewarding like the *Lieh Tzu* or *Chuang Tzu*. I get no pleasure, and wonder why continue? I haven't written a poem in a year. The last novel I completed was between three and four years ago and I have no interest in writing another. I don't have the drive, the stomach for it. Perhaps I have nothing more to say. In three weeks, I will turn sixty-five. Thirty-five years ago, I could think of nothing but writing—and everything—the music, reading, community, publishing, rewards, notoriety, art, lifestyle that went along with it—they meant the world. Now I feel as if I have been kicked in the stomach so hard that I will never breathe the same way again. It seems there are more writers now than ever, at least in my lifetime. Everywhere little presses and big presses and online magazines and prizes and more new books than I could ever read and poets posting poems on social media and performing at poetry slams. There are countless people young and old that feel the way I felt all those years ago. Poets with high self-esteem host workshops in their homes and charge people admission, writing conferences and retreats thrive at exotic locations, MFA programs boom and in the book store shelves full of new writers and old writers and when one of them dies we mourn their greatness but there are five more to take their place. If I want to read anything now it is poetry from close friends, or poets from ancient China or William Carlos Williams or to reread a Melville or Twain or Virginia Woolf novel. I don't want to read a first book from a promising new novelist or debut book of poems from a recently graduated MFA student. I have little urge to write poems or fiction of my own. I want to relax and think about dying and learn how to die. That's been on my mind for the past couple of years. Studying the Tao, practicing yoga, the unification of mind, body, universe. Sometimes friends ask me *What have you been up to?* When I tell them, *I am getting ready to die* they look at me as if I am somehow mad or planning to kill myself. But it's not that. If you have a good life, there should be a good death. It's all one. And it's all nothing. Surely it won't be that much longer and if I am not ready that would be failure. How do I leave everything behind, return to the nothing from which I emerged? What does it mean all the characters I created, words that made experiences some of which I have doubted I wrote since I penned them? Where the hundreds and hundreds of students who took creative writing classes or "studied" literature with me? To what end? Where have they gone? What have they done? Where does all the music I have listened to go, paintings I have viewed, books I have read, movies I have watched, hikes I have taken, mushrooms I have foraged, friends and family I have loved, meals I have enjoyed, drugs and alcohol I have consumed—tears and joys the vast majority of which I cannot recall? I am a pop in a timeless chamber—look for me where water winds its way.

Some Other PFP/AJAR Contemporaries Titles

A Four-Sided Bed - Elizabeth Searle

Big City Cat: My Life in Folk Rock - Steve Forbert

Fighting Gravity - Peggy Rambach

Girl to Girl: The Real Deal on Being A Girl Today
- Anne Driscoll

Lunch with Buddha - Roland Merullo

Make A Wish But Not For Money
- Suzanne Strempek Shea

Music In and On the Air - Lloyd Schwartz

My Ground Trilogy - Joseph Torra

Smedley's Secret Guide to World Literature
- Askold Melnyczuk

The Calling - Sterling Watson

The Return - Roland Merullo

*The Winding Stream: The Carters, the Cashes and
the Course of Country Music* - Beth Harrington

*Talk Show: On the Couch
with Contemporary Writers*- Jaime Clarke

*This is Paradise: An Irish Mother's Grief,
an African Village's Plight and the Medical Clinic
That Brought Fresh Hope to Both*
- Suzanne Strempek Shea

Tornado Alley - Craig Nova

Waking Slow - Ioanna Opidee

CPSIA information can be obtained
at www.ICGtesting.com
Printed in the USA
FSHW021655260521
81727FS